NEW PENGUIN SHAKESPEARE
GENERAL EDITOR: T. J. B. SPENCER
ASSOCIATE EDITOR: STANLEY WELLS

WILLIAM SHAKESPEARE

*

THE WINTER'S TALE

EDITED BY
ERNEST SCHANZER

PENGUIN BOOKS

PENGUIN BOOKS

Published by the Penguin Group
Penguin Books Ltd, 27 Wrights Lane, London W8 5TZ, England
Penguin Putnam Inc., 375 Hudson Street, New York, New York 10014, USA
Penguin Books Australia Ltd, Ringwood, Victoria, Australia
Penguin Books Canada Ltd, 10 Alcorn Avenue, Toronto, Ontario, Canada M4V 3B2
Penguin Books India (P) Ltd, 11, Community Centre, Panchsheel Park, New Delhi – 110 017, India
Penguin Books (NZ) Ltd, Private Bag 102902, NSMC, Auckland, New Zealand
Penguin Books (South Africa) (Pty) Ltd, 5 Watkins Street, Denver Ext 4, Johannesburg 2094, South Af

Penguin Books Ltd, Registered Offices: Harmondsworth, Middlesex, England

First published 1986
10

Printed in England by Clays Ltd, St Ives plc
Set in Monophoto Photina

CONTENTS

INTRODUCTION

'THE WINTER'S TALE' is one of Shakespeare's comedy titles – other notable instances are 'A Midsummer Night's Dream' and 'Measure for Measure' – the meaning of which is not simple and single but complex and elusive. In the popular usage of his day 'a winter's tale' meant a fantastic tale, especially a ghost story. It is to such a tale that Lady Macbeth alludes, when she tells her husband, who has just seen a *real* ghost:

> *O, these flaws and starts,*
> *Impostors to true fear, would well become*
> *A woman's story at a winter's fire,*
> *Authorized by her grandam.*
>
> Macbeth, III.4.62–5

The main intention of the title may therefore be to emphasize that this play tells an incredible story. And this emphasis is renewed at its most incredible moments, in the last Act. Upon the reunion of father and daughter one of Leontes's courtiers is made to declare: 'This news, which is called true, is so like an old tale that the verity of it is in strong suspicion' (V.2.27–9). And in the final scene Paulina says of Hermione:

> *That she is living,*
> *Were it but told you, should be hooted at*
> *Like an old tale.*   V.3.115–17

It has been claimed that the purpose of these references is to remind us of the story's unreality, to break the dramatic

7

illusion, and thus keep the audience detached and critical. But is not its effect rather the opposite: to heighten our sense of the story's reality, to make us feel that what we are witnessing on the stage is life, which is stranger than fiction? When we introduce some true account with the words 'Something quite incredible happened to me the other day', we seek to strengthen our listeners' *belief*, not their disbelief. And the same seems to have been Shakespeare's purpose in devising the play's title and in likening its most marvellous events to an old tale.

Yet by calling his play not '*A* Winter's Tale' but '*The* Winter's Tale' he may have wanted to refer us to the tale told by Leontes's little son, Mamillius, at the opening of Act II. Begged by his mother to tell her a tale, he asks:

> *Merry or sad shall't be?*

HERMIONE
> *As merry as you will.*

MAMILLIUS
> *A sad tale's best for winter. I have one*
> *Of sprites and goblins.*

HERMIONE *Let's have that, good sir.*
> *Come on, sit down; come on, and do your best*
> *To fright me with your sprites. You're powerful at it.*

MAMILLIUS
> *There was a man –*

HERMIONE *Nay, come sit down; then on.*

MAMILLIUS
> *Dwelt by a churchyard – I will tell it softly:*
> *Yond crickets shall not hear it.*

HERMIONE *Come on, then,*
> *And give't me in mine ear.* II.1.23–32

By the end of the third Act we have come to realize that the winter's tale Mamillius begins to tell mirrors that of the play. Leontes has become the man who dwelt by a church-yard, and even of the sprites and goblins we have had a glimpse in the vision of Antigonus (III.3.15-36). By calling his play 'The Winter's Tale' Shakespeare may have wanted to make us think of Mamillius's tale, seen as an emblem of the play's main events.

But this still does not exhaust the possible significances of the title. The play's story is not only a fantastic and incredible tale, as well as the sad and frightening tale best suited for winter that Mamillius begins to tell. It is also a tale which is principally *about* winter, the winter which Leontes creates within him and around him. Throughout his dramatic career Shakespeare was fond of drawing on the symbolism of the four seasons. For instance, the opening lines of *Richard III*:

> *Now is the winter of our discontent*
> *Made glorious summer by this sun of York,*
> *And all the clouds that loured upon our house*
> *In the deep bosom of the ocean buried . . .*
>
> *Richard III*, I.1.1-4

describe a progression very similar to that of *The Winter's Tale*. But only in our play is this symbolism made one of the chief vehicles of its significances and one of the main determinants of its structure. To underline this may have been a part of Shakespeare's intention in calling his play 'The Winter's Tale'.

*

On 15 May 1611 Simon Forman, a quack-doctor and astrologer, went to the Globe theatre and there saw a performance of *The Winter's Tale*. His summary of its plot, which has been preserved among his papers, is remarkable for the absence of any mention of the statue-scene and for the lively interest in Autolycus's tricks, from which he derived the moral 'beware of trusting feigned beggars or fawning fellows'. The performance which Forman saw is likely to have been among the first, for the scanty evidence we possess points to its having been written not many months earlier.

Shakespeare based his play on one of the most popular pieces of Elizabethan prose fiction, Robert Greene's *Pandosto*, which, first published in 1588, was reprinted in 1592, 1595, and 1607, and went through at least fourteen more editions before the end of the seventeenth century. Greene seems to have invented its story, taking for his model the Greek romances, prose tales written in the first centuries A.D., and favourite reading with the Elizabethans. They were stories of marvellous adventures, marked by the separation of lovers; an abundance of shipwrecks; hairbreadth escapes from wild beasts, bandits, or pirates; all ending happily in miraculous reunions of parents and children, or lovers, long believed dead.

In rewriting the second half of *Pericles*, some three years before *The Winter's Tale*, Shakespeare had already used a story derived from Greek romance and highly representative of it, not only in its plot, which is a tissue of incidents typical of the *genre*, but also in its location (Greece and the Eastern Mediterranean) and in the Greek names of most of its characters. In *Pandosto* Shakespeare found a story which in its location (the kingdoms of Bohemia and Sicilia) does not betray its origin in Greek romance, and some of the characters of which bear names that are not Greek. Only Apollo's oracle on the island of Delphos points unmistakably to the story's literary ancestry. It is remarkable that Shakespeare, in adapting it, brought it closer to the world of Greek romance. He did so partly by giving Greek names to the characters which he renamed or added. Greene's Pandosto became Leontes, his Bellaria Hermione, his Egistus Polixenes. Antigonus, Dion, Cleomenes, Archidamus are all names introduced by Shakespeare, and culled from his great storehouse of Greek names, Plutarch's *Lives*. The only name Shakespeare took over from *Pandosto* is the Greek name Mopsa: in the novel it belongs to the shrewish wife of the shepherd, in the play to one of the young shepherdesses. Even his Bohemian rogue is given the Greek name Autolycus, in violation of Shakespeare's practice of bestowing English names upon his comic low-life characters, whatever country they belong to.

But it was chiefly by means of some of the main changes made in the plot of *Pandosto* that Shakespeare brought it closer to the world of Greek romance. The most fundamental of these changes is the 'resurrection' of Hermione. In *Pandosto* the slandered Queen dies and remains dead. The King, sixteen years later, re-enacts his earlier tyranny in his treatment of his daughter, for whom, ignorant of her identity, he is smitten with violent love. Then, after a brief period of joy which follows upon the recognition, he suddenly commits suicide. Through this unhappy close *Pandosto* deviates from the story-pattern of Greek romance, in which, often miraculously, against all odds, a happy ending concludes the long tale of suffering. And it similarly departs from the pattern of Shakespeare's romantic comedies, of which the same holds true. Had he adhered to the ending of *Pandosto*, he would have written a play unlike any of his other comedies, in all of which the protagonist, however guilty, is dismissed to happiness, repentant and reformed. Neither would it have fitted the pattern of his tragedies, in most of which not only the protagonist but also several other main characters are left dead when the curtain falls. The happy ending of

The Winter's Tale thus makes the plot conform not only to the conventions of Greek romance but also to those of Shakespeare's comedies. He might, of course, have given the story a happy ending without resurrecting Hermione. This is done in a verse-adaptation of *Pandosto*, Francis Sabie's *The Fisherman's Tale* (1595), which, because of a number of very minor coincidences, has been claimed as one of the secondary sources of *The Winter's Tale*. Sabie, like Shakespeare, omits the King's incestuous love for his daughter, and makes the story end amid universal happiness but without resurrecting the Queen. Yet even such an ending would have made *The Winter's Tale* unique among Shakespeare's comedies, none of which includes the death of a central character who is a model of virtue. It was quite another matter to leave minor characters, such as Mamillius and Antigonus, unresurrected. But the Queen had to be kept alive if the play was to conform to the pattern of Shakespeare's romantic comedies.

In dramatizing the 'resurrection' of Hermione, he evidently drew on memories of two of his own previous plays, *Much Ado About Nothing* and *Pericles*. The plot-parallels between *The Winter's Tale* and *Much Ado About Nothing* are the more extensive: in both plays the husband (or bridegroom) publicly accuses his wife (or bride) of unchastity; she falls into a swoon and is believed to be dead by all who are present; but she recovers, and is secretly hidden away, while her husband (or bridegroom) continues to believe her to be dead. He discovers her innocence, repents of his actions, devises an epitaph for her tomb, setting forth the cause of her death, and vows to visit that tomb as an act of penance (daily in *The Winter's Tale*, once a year in *Much Ado About Nothing*). He promises – and here Shakespeare drew on memories of Bandello's *novella*, his source for *Much Ado About Nothing*, rather than on the play itself – that when he marries again he will only take a wife chosen for him (by the slandered woman's father in the one case, her friend in the other). One further hint Shakespeare may have derived from the *novella*. Describing the slandered woman lying in her swoon, Bandello remarks that she resembled a marble statue rather than a live woman. This may have suggested the idea of making Hermione pose as her own statue (a not uncommon motif in narrative and dramatic romance).

In the shaping of the statue-scene memories of the finale of *Pericles* played a major part. In both plays a queen is believed to be dead and buried (in *Pericles* she is put into a coffin and cast into the sea). But she returns to life and remains in seclusion for many years (fourteen in the one play, sixteen in the other). The final scene depicts her reunion, after this long gap of time, with husband and daughter, who had both firmly believed her to be dead. In both plays this scene breathes a similar atmosphere of ceremonious solemnity turning to wonder and joy; in both the daughter kneels before her mother, who calls her 'my own'.

The romance motif of the woman who appears to have died but returns to life seems to have had a special fascination for Shakespeare. Apart from the plays already mentioned, he had used it as early as *Romeo and Juliet* (where the return to life is, however, of the utmost brevity) and as late as *Cymbeline*. What makes its treatment in *The Winter's Tale* unique is the fact that the playwright has not taken the audience into his confidence, but has made it share the wonder experienced by Leontes, Polixenes, and Perdita at Hermione's 'resurrection'. It is true that the first two scenes of Act V contain a few hints that she may be still alive. In V.1.73–5 Paulina makes Leontes swear never to marry again,

> *Unless another,*
> *As like Hermione as is her picture*
> *Affront his eye ...*

and immediately upon this tells him,

> *Yet if my lord will marry – if you will, sir,*
> *No remedy, but you will – give me the office*
> *To choose you a queen: she shall not be so young*
> *As was your former, but she shall be such*
> *As, walked your first queen's ghost, it should take joy*
> *To see her in your arms.*

LEONTES   *My true Paulina,*
We shall not marry till thou bid'st us.

PAULINA   *That*
Shall be when your first queen's again in breath;
Never till then.   V.1.76–84

Here a suspicion that she is still alive may begin to stir in
us. And this suspicion may become more fully roused by
the Second Gentleman's report in the following scene
(V.2.103–5) that Paulina 'hath privately, twice or thrice a
day, ever since the death of Hermione, visited that removed
house' where the statue stands. Yet few spectators who
are new to the play will approach the statue-scene with
anything but a conviction of Hermione's death. For at the
end of Act III Shakespeare had gone out of his way to
instil such a conviction. Not only had Paulina, who has
been established to the audience as a thoroughly trust-
worthy and truthful character, sworn it:

> *I say she's dead; I'll swear't. If word nor oath*
> *Prevail not, go and see. If you can bring*
> *Tincture or lustre in her lip, her eye,*
> *Heat outwardly or breath within, I'll serve you*
> *As I would do the gods.*   III.2.201–5

But Antigonus, who had left Sicilia before the trial and could therefore have no knowledge of Hermione's supposed death, tells us, just before he is eaten by the bear, of a strange vision in which her ghost appeared to him and from which he infers that she must have died (III.3.15–45). There is no precedent in Elizabethan drama for the spirit of a living person appearing to others either in dream or waking.

All this has led some commentators to maintain that the idea of resurrecting Hermione did not come to Shakespeare until after he had finished the third Act, his original plan having been to end the play with the reunion of Leontes, Perdita, and Polixenes. It is an attractive theory, but it fails to convince, chiefly for the reason already given: a Hermione left dead at the end of the play would have made *The Winter's Tale* unique among Shakespeare's comedies. Besides, it is hard to believe that, had such a change of plan occurred, he would have failed to bring what he had already written into line with his usual practice by inserting, towards the end of Act III, a brief scene between Hermione and Paulina, which informed the audience of her recovery and sequestration.

It is preferable to assume that what is unique in *The Winter's Tale* is not the plot-pattern as originally planned but Shakespeare's decision not to take the audience into his confidence. His habitual practice – in contrast to that of many other playwrights – had been to put the audience in full possession of all relevant knowledge, so that, even on a first viewing, the dramatic irony that derives from the characters' lack of this knowledge is immediately felt. Towards the end of his career Shakespeare seems to have become willing at times to sacrifice dramatic irony in order to startle his audience or make them share the sense of wonder experienced by the characters in the play. The first signs of this desire to startle his audience appear in *Cymbeline*, the play which was probably written just before *The Winter's Tale*. There, contrary to his previous practice, Shakespeare has kept the audience ignorant of Iachimo's plans, so that the first time they see the play many spectators experience a shock of surprise and horror when he emerges from the trunk in Imogen's bedchamber. In *The Winter's Tale* Shakespeare goes further, not merely declining to pass on to his audience a vital piece of knowledge, but, through Paulina's speech and the vision of Antigonus, leading them utterly astray.

The effect of Shakespeare's main departure from the plot of *Pandosto* in resurrecting Hermione was to bring the play closer to the world of Greek romance, not only in the happy ending it provides but also in the way in which the reunion is staged: the romance motif of a statue impersonated by a living woman believed dead, the sacrifice of psychological verisimilitude to theatrical effect (for looked at realistically the role Hermione is made to play in the statue-scene must seem intolerable), the subordination of everything else to the rousing of a feeling of wonder – all this is characteristic of Greek romance.

Shakespeare's other main departure from the plot of *Pandosto* had a similar effect. In the novel the baby daughter is placed in a boat and left to the mercy of the waves. After being tossed for two days in a terrible storm, the little boat is driven ashore on the coast of Sicilia, where Egistus (Shakespeare's Polixenes) is king. There the child is found and adopted by a shepherd. These events, easy to narrate in a novel, would have been difficult to stage. By inventing Antigonus, and having him leave the child in 'some remote and desert place', as Leontes had made him swear, Shakespeare made the story not only more suited to the stage but also more credible. Besides, he brought it closer to Greek romance by adding three motifs absent in the novel: the vision of Antigonus, the shipwreck of the mariners, and the bear. Dream visions in which goddesses prophesy and impose commands are the stock-in-trade of Greek romance. So are shipwrecks and sudden attacks of wild beasts. Having invented Antigonus and made him leave the child in 'the deserts of Bohemia', Shakespeare had to kill him off, and with him all the mariners; for it was essential that none of them should return to Sicilia, able to tell the penitent King where his child might be. To the question asked by one critic why, in the name of economy, Shakespeare did not engulf Antigonus with the rest, but made him meet a separate death on land, the answer would seem to be twofold: firstly, Shakespeare wanted to leave his audience in no doubt of Antigonus's death (ship-wrecked persons in romance are apt to survive and return to their country); and secondly, he wanted to introduce the bear. For it served several purposes: on the one hand, it is a dramatic embodiment of all the perils which beset Perdita, and fills us with pity and fear for her; on the other, the sight of an actor in a bear's skin – for it was almost certainly not a real bear which was used by Shakespeare's company – pursuing Antigonus across the stage was bound to have a partly comic effect. That this effect was intentional is shown by the way in which, some twenty lines later, the Clown is made to narrate the double calamity of the death of Antigonus and the drowning of the mariners (see Commentary on III.3.81–102). Being forced by the exigencies of his plot to kill them off, Shakespeare evidently took pains to make their deaths as un-lamentable as possible.

Shakespeare's decision to introduce the bear may be responsible for another minor change he made in dramatizing *Pandosto*. In the novel Pandosto, who corresponds to

Leontes, is King of Bohemia; and Egistus, who corresponds to Polixenes, is King of Sicilia. Shakespeare
transposed this, so that all the action which in the novel is
placed in Bohemia is in the play located in Sicilia, and vice
versa. It may well have been the thought that the sea-
coast of Bohemia seems a more suitable habitat for a bear
than that of Sicilia which principally determined him to
make the switch. Another consideration may have been the
wish to locate his sheep-shearing feast in Bohemia in
order to keep it free from the intrusion of misleading or
irrelevant conceptions of Sicilian pastoral life, with which
the more educated part of his audience were familiar from
their reading of the classics. The transposition may also
have been unconsciously aided by the fact that *Much Ado
About Nothing*, which, as we have seen, was much in
Shakespeare's mind while reshaping the plot of *Pandosto*,
is his only other play with a Sicilian setting.

Some commentators speak of Antigonus as becoming
guilty in carrying out the King's command to expose the
child, and see his death as a punishment for allowing himself to become an accessary to the crime. But this is not
how Shakespeare presents the matter. He depicts him as an
entirely upright, humane, and honourable old courtier, who
carries out the command in fulfilment of a solemn oath,
and as an alternative to seeing the child 'instantly consumed with fire'. Failure to perform it would lead not only
to his own death but also to that of his wife (II.3.169–72).
Shakespeare could not have been more careful to keep
Antigonus free from guilt in the exposure of the child.

While his deviation from the plot of *Pandosto* in having
the babe left 'in some remote and desert place' led to the
creation of Antigonus, his deviation from it in resurrecting
Hermione led to that of Paulina, who was needed to act as
'presenter' in the statue-scene. With this role she is made

to combine a quite different one: that of the devoted servant, who, by means of blunt plain-speaking, tries to restore her master to his senses. It is a role remarkably like that of Kent in *King Lear*. In each case we have a servant of a king, who, seeing him denounce and reject the woman who entirely loves him and is a pattern of all virtues, accuses the king of madness and claims to be his physician, who would cure him of his diseased opinion, but is brutally spurned by him. And each takes loving care of him in his phase of penitent suffering, after his insane delusion has been dispelled.

A character who has no counterpart in *Pandosto*, but whose introduction is not due to any requirements of the altered plot, is Autolycus. His part in advancing the plot is, indeed, minimal: it is virtually confined to getting the old Shepherd and his son on board the ship which takes them to Sicilia, where they are needed for the identification of Perdita. Shakespeare could easily have devised some other means of getting them on to the ship. He wanted Autolycus above all as a purveyor of the laughter and songs which pervade the Bohemian country-scenes and serve as a contrast to the wintry gloom which the actions of Leontes have created at his court.

Looked at astrologically – and Shakespeare encourages us to look at him in this way – Autolycus is 'mercurial man', a compendium of the traits which the planet Mercury was thought to produce in those who came under its influence. These traits are summed up by Mercury himself in John Lyly's *Woman in the Moon* (IV.1.8–11), when he is made to declare

> *Now is Pandora in my regiment,*
> *And I will make her false and full of sleights,*
> *Thievish, lying, subtle, eloquent,*
> *For these alone belong to Mercury.*

Renaissance hand-books on astrology for the most part bear out this list. For instance, William Lilly, in his *Christian Astrology* (1647), claims Mercury to be 'the author of subtlety, tricks, devices, perjury, etc.', making anyone coming under his influence 'a great liar . . . cheating and thieving everywhere' (pages 48–9). Autolycus himself jestingly attributes his and his father's propensity for stealing to the influence of the planet Mercury: 'My father named me Autolycus, who, being, as I am, littered under Mercury, was likewise a snapper-up of unconsidered trifles' (IV.3.24–6). However, it is by no means purely the unprepossessing qualities belonging to 'mercurial man' that Autolycus exhibits, but also the more attractive ones: sprightliness, volatility, a ready wit, a love of music, and an aptitude for commerce. Yet Autolycus is no mere astrological paradigm, nor a social document (as which he has sometimes been treated), but one of Shakespeare's most vivid and entertaining creations.

Another character who has no counterpart in *Pandosto* is the Clown. In the novel the shepherd is alone when he discovers the child, and carries it home to his shrewish wife. Shakespeare evidently found that he had no need for the wife, but that he had to create a companion for the shepherd, with whom he could share the discovery. The result was the Clown, a masterpiece of comic portraiture. His attitudes and responses are carefully contrasted with those of his father, a contrast that is brought out most clearly in their way of responding to the good fortune that befalls them at the end of the play (see Commentary on V.2.148). They are the third pair of father and son that Shakespeare has created in *The Winter's Tale*. But here the contrast between the two generations takes a very different form from that between Leontes and Mamillius, Polixenes and Florizel, and one by no means favourable to the young.

It is the old Shepherd, representative of the traditional rustic virtues, whom we are made to love and admire, while his son, no emblem of a golden world of innocence, is shown to be made of a much cheaper metal.

*

Not only did Shakespeare create a number of characters who have no counterpart in *Pandosto*; he also radically transformed some of the main characters he derived from it. The prime example is Leontes. There is, first of all, Shakespeare's treatment of his jealousy. In *Pandosto* it is depicted as a passion which grows gradually in the King, over a long period of time, and is nourished by such actions of the Queen as her frequent visits to the bed-chamber of Egistus 'to see that nothing should be amiss to mislike him', actions which, though wholly innocent, yet provide solid ground for Pandosto's suspicions. Shakespeare, on the contrary, shows the jealousy of Leontes flaring up quite suddenly, in the course of I.2, descending like a terrible dream, and vanishing just as suddenly when the shock of the news of the death of Mamillius restores him to his senses; so that it has been compared to the fits of divinely inspired frenzy that afflict some of the heroes of Greek tragedy. He depicts Leontes as a man who is just as far removed as Othello from the traditional stage-figure of the jealous husband (neither Paulina nor anyone else ever accuses him of being by nature jealous), yet who, without any super-subtle villain to deceive him, becomes persuaded in the course of a few hundred lines that his beloved wife has committed adultery with his dearest friend. Faced with such an apparent flouting of psycho-logical verisimilitude, some critics have tried to approximate the jealousy of Leontes to that of Pandosto by claiming that Shakespeare meant it to be seen as a gradual growth and that he is therefore to be acted as being already in the grips of jealousy when he makes his first appearance on the stage, while his urging Polixenes to stay is to be understood as the device of jealousy seeking proof. There are several powerful reasons for rejecting this notion. It would be something quite new in Shakespeare's dramaturgy to leave the establishment of such an important point entirely to the actor, without inserting one word, in soliloquy or aside, to make it plain to the audience. Next, it would destroy what Shakespeare seems evidently at pains to communicate to us in the first hundred lines of the scene: the image of the King's entirely happy relationship with wife, son, and friend, of the Paradise which is lost through his insane delusion. And finally it goes against another image which the play as a whole seems concerned to establish (as we shall see more clearly when looking at the structure of *The Winter's Tale*): that of the suddenness with which the blasts of winter blight the blossoms of spring and summer, an expression of the precariousness of human happiness. To convey this Shakespeare had to show the sudden descent of the blight into a smiling, unclouded summer landscape. And yet in order to remain within the bounds of psychological realism he had to motivate its descent at that particular point in the scene. In their search for such motivation some critics have fastened on Hermione's words to Polixenes:

> *Th'offences we have made you do we'll answer,*
> *If you first sinned with us, and that with us*
> *You did continue fault, and that you slipped not*
> *With any but with us.*   I.2.83–6

These lines, they think, are overheard by Leontes out of their context, so that he takes them to be a confession of having sinned with Polixenes, Hermione using the royal plural. It is an ingenious explanation, yet it also will not do. It is unbelievable that at this crucial point Shakespeare would not have given Leontes a word to utter which would have conveyed his misapprehension to the audience. And when, some twenty lines later, he is made to vent for the first time his suspicions in an aside, there is no hint here, or in anything he says later, that he has overheard what he takes to be a confession of adultery. On the contrary, the speech expresses his doubts whether Hermione's entertainment of Polixenes is perfectly innocent or not:

> *This entertainment*
> *May a free face put on, derive a liberty*
> *From heartiness, from bounty, fertile bosom,*
> *And well become the agent – 't may, I grant.*
> *But to be paddling palms and pinching fingers,*
> *As now they are, and making practised smiles*
> *As in a looking glass; and then to sigh, as 'twere*
> *The mort o'th'deer – O, that is entertainment*
> *My bosom likes not, nor my brows!*   I.2.111–19

If Shakespeare's dramaturgy here is to conform with his previous practice, the incident that sets off this speech must be found in the lines immediately preceding it. And this is, I believe, precisely where we do find it, though, very strangely, it has escaped the notice of commentators.

When Leontes hears from Hermione that Polixenes is willing to stay, he tells her that only once before has she spoken to better purpose. Urged by her to say when this was, he declares:

> *Why, that was when*
> *Three crabbèd months had soured themselves to death*
> *Ere I could make thee open thy white hand*
> *And clap thyself my love: then didst thou utter*
> *'I am yours for ever'.*

23

HERMIONE   *'Tis Grace indeed.*
  Why, lo you know, I have spoke to th'purpose twice:
  The one for ever earned a royal husband;
  Th'other for some while a friend.   I.2.101–8

'Friend' in Elizabethan usage commonly means 'lover'. Hermione's unfortunate formulation, her way of paralleling the two occasions, her use of the word 'friend', the sight of her once again opening her white hand and giving it to Polixenes (as shown by line 115), all this works together to cause a sudden flare-up of suspicion in Leontes, a man who, like Othello, is 'not easily jealous' and needed this particular conjunction of malign circumstances to make him become so. As with Othello, suspicion, once kindled, grows within a few hundred lines into a settled conviction of his wife's guilt. But in contrast with the Moor, his love for his wife does not continue, but soon gives way to hate. There is no inner conflict between love for her and a wish for revenge, only the urge to destroy her in order to regain his peace of mind (II.3.2–9).

Like Othello, he suffers two tragic experiences which are recurrent in Shakespeare's plays: that of disillusion with the person dearest to him, when he becomes falsely persuaded of Hermione's worthlessness; and that of discovering that in his blind folly he has done things which shut him off for ever from all hopes of happiness. This last experience is even more agonizing than that of Othello since he has no Iago to blame for his misfortunes. Alone among Shakespeare's tragic figures he is solely self-deceived, and not also deceived by others.

In contrast with Pandosto, whose belief in the Queen's guilt comes to be shared by the people when they hear of the sudden flight of Egistus and Franion (the counterpart of Camillo), Shakespeare shows how Leontes becomes utterly isolated, no arguments or abuse succeeding in making others share his delusions. Why he should have chosen to impair this image by making Antigonus confess to a belief in Hermione's guilt just before his death (III.3.42–5) is one of the puzzles for which no ready answer is available.

In the first half of the play Leontes still bears some resemblance to his counterpart in the novel. In the second half the two characters cease to have anything in common. Upon the arrival of the young lovers in his kingdom Pandosto reiterates his former evil by tyrannically casting the innocent prince into prison in order to have him out of the way while attempting to make his daughter, Fawnia, his mistress. When he finds her firm against all promises and threats, his love for her turns to hatred, so that he is quite ready to carry out the request of Egistus to have her put to death. Nothing could be more of a contrast with Leontes, who, after sixteen years of penance for his crimes, is shown to be all goodness, humility, and courtesy. While Pandosto's re-enactment of it sixteen years later makes his cruel behaviour towards his queen seem something rooted in his nature, that of Leontes is made to seem a unique and short-lived aberration, a solitary fit of insane delusion during which he becomes utterly transformed, a stranger to his true self.

Shakespeare is evidently anxious to retain our sympathy for Leontes even at the height of his tyrannical ravings. He does so chiefly by means of his soliloquies and asides, in which we are allowed to have insight into the growth of his delusion and are made to participate in his suffering. As in so many of his plays (for instance, the opening scene of *King Lear*) Shakespeare creates a double vista by making us share both the crazed vision of the King and the sane vision of those around him. In II.3 he shows how Paulina's arrival with the child at that precise moment and the well-meant but ill-chosen words she uses to make him accept his paternity of it lead naturally and inevitably to the cruel doom which the plot required him to pronounce. Having never allowed us to lose our sympathy with Leontes, Shakespeare has no difficulty in gaining our affection for him as soon as he becomes freed from his delusion.

The transformation of the novel's young lovers is less profound than that of Pandosto, but still far-reaching. Greene's young prince, Dorastus, is ashamed of his love for the shepherdess Fawnia and tries his utmost to resist it. Like his father (and Polixenes) he sees it as dishonour-able, disgraceful, calamitous. Only because he finds his love stronger than his sense of 'honour' does he finally yield to it and, after Fawnia refuses to become his mistress, offer to make her his wife. Nothing could be further re-moved from Florizel's exaltation of Perdita above any princess, his total unconcern about her social station, his declaration that

> were I crowned the most imperial monarch,
> Thereof most worthy, were I the fairest youth
> That ever made eye swerve, had force and knowledge
> More than was ever man's, I would not prize them
> Without her love; for her employ them all;
> Commend them and condemn them to her service
> Or to their own perdition.   IV.4.369–75

Fawnia's thoughts, when she finds herself in love with the Prince, also dwell mainly on the difference of rank between them. Where for Perdita 'the difference forges dread' (IV.4.17) because it threatens the continuance of their relationship, Fawnia sees her love for the Prince as a violation of the order of nature, and therefore likely to have dire consequences. As she is preoccupied with social

rank, what pleases her most about the projected marriage
to Dorastus is the thought of one day becoming queen.
Hence it does not come as a surprise that when, at the end
of the novel, she discovers the man who has been treating
her and her lover in the most villainous fashion to be her
father, we are told (apparently without the least touch of
irony): 'Fawnia was not more joyful that she had found
such a father than Dorastus was glad he should get such a
wife.' We are worlds away from Perdita, with her

> *I was not much afeard; for once or twice*
> *I was about to speak and tell him plainly,*
> *The selfsame sun that shines upon his court*
> *Hides not his visage from our cottage, but*
> *Looks on alike.*   IV.4.439–43

Much as he has done with Leontes, Shakespeare has made
the young lovers far more attractive and lovable than are
their counterparts in *Pandosto*.

The conflict between love and honour which afflicts
Dorastus is only one of many such conflicts experienced by
characters in the novel. Fawnia is divided between her
love for the Prince and her fear of the ill consequences of
such a presumptuous passion; Pandosto's servant Franion
between the desire for the rewards to be gained by poison-
ing Egistus and the prompting of his conscience; Pandosto
himself between his 'frantic affection' for Fawnia and his
awareness of its vileness; even the shepherd between
the desire for the gold found with the child and fear of the
consequences of keeping it. Of all these conflicts Shakespeare takes over only Fawnia's, and even that he barely
glances at (in IV.4.17–40). The others he has no use for.
As he had made Florizel, Camillo, and the old Shepherd
so much nobler and more lovable than their counterparts
in the novel, there was, indeed, no room for them.

Greene's concern in portraying these conflicts was rhetorical rather than psychological. For him they were opportunities for writing neatly balanced, elaborately patterned speeches through which he wanted to impress his readers with his juggler's skill in playing with words, rather than with his knowledge of the human heart. This lack of concern with the creation of living characters was not shared by Shakespeare. The claim has sometimes been made that *The Winter's Tale*, along with the other Last Plays, shows a loss of interest in the idiosyncrasies of human nature; that, in conformity with the requirements of romance, or in order to become fitter vehicles for symbolic significances, its characters have been purposely made shadowy, flat, undifferentiated. Leontes, Hermione, Florizel and Perdita, the old Shepherd and his son, Autolycus and Paulina bear firm witness against this claim. They are as intensely realized, as carefully distinguished, endowed with as individual an utterance as any characters in Shakespeare's previous plays. It is true that some of them, notably Leontes and Perdita, are also vehicles of symbolic significances. But so are Lear and Cordelia, or Macbeth and Duncan. Whatever may be true of the other Last Plays, there is nothing that marks off Shakespeare's treatment of characters in *The Winter's Tale* from that in his mature comedies and tragedies.

*

It has been suggested (by E. M. W. Tillyard) that we may see in *The Winter's Tale* the whole scheme of Dante's *Divine Comedy* compressed into a single play. This is true if we regard it as centring on the spiritual journey of Leontes. In Acts I–III we are given the *Inferno*, the hell which he builds in his own mind. Like that of Milton's Satan, it is a hell which is created and sustained entirely by

himself. Next, at the end of Act III and the beginning of
Act V, we are given glimpses of the *Purgatorio*, the sixteen-
year period of repentance and penance. And finally, in the
remainder of Act V, we have the *Paradiso* in his reunion
with daughter, wife, and friend. For the broad outlines of
this pattern Shakespeare seems to have turned back to
Cymbeline. There he had depicted in Posthumus a husband
who mistakenly believes his wife to have been unfaithful
to him, and who goes through a mental hell (much more
briefly sketched than in *The Winter's Tale*), which is
quickly followed by a period of repentance and penance,
until the final joyful reunion with his wife. (Incidentally,
The Winter's Tale also follows *Cymbeline* in another triple
division: in beginning at the court; then moving into the
country, where the King's children, living a simple existence, without princely nurture, yet display their princely
nature; and ending again at court, amidst joyful reunions
and reconciliations.)

This tripartite division of the play into *Inferno*, *Purgatorio*, and *Paradiso* involves, however, a simplification of
its structural pattern, for it takes no account of Act IV,
which is almost as long as the first three Acts put together.
In it Leontes does not appear at all, and instead our attention centres on Perdita. This double focus, upon the
father in the first three Acts and upon his daughter in
Act IV, is found in only one other play by Shakespeare,
Pericles, which, in fact, provided its chief structural
model.

In both plays the centre of the stage is held in the first
three Acts by the royal father (Pericles, Leontes); between
Acts III and IV are placed the great gaps of time (fourteen
and sixteen years); in Act IV the father does not appear,
while our attention focuses on the daughter (Marina,
Perdita), whom we last saw just after her birth in the first

part of the play; in the final Act the two focuses unite, with the reunion of father and daughter, followed by that of husband and wife (Thaisa, Hermione), whom the husband had believed dead and buried. In both plays the reunion of father and daughter is the result of mere chance, while that of husband and wife is the result of direction, its agent being the goddess Diana in the one play, Paulina in the other.

Shakespeare often gives his main character a long rest about three-quarters of the way through the play (as in *Hamlet* or *Macbeth*). But only in *Pericles* and *The Winter's Tale* is there this double focus, with the protagonist of the first three Acts not appearing in Act IV, his place being taken by a completely new character. And nowhere else is there a similar treatment of time, with a gap of many years placed in the middle of the play. Elsewhere in his comedies Shakespeare either observed the most rigorous unity of time (as in *The Comedy of Errors* and *The Tempest*) or allowed at most several months to elapse in the course of the action (as, for instance, in *All's Well that Ends Well* and *Cymbeline*).

In both *Pericles* and *The Winter's Tale* the relation between the two halves of the play is one of contrast as well as of likeness. But in *The Winter's Tale* the contrasts are much more pervasive and important than in *Pericles*. Indeed, they are a principal way in which Shakespeare communicates the play's 'meaning' to the audience.

He has divided it into a predominantly destructive half and a predominantly creative and restorative half; into a winter half, centring on the desolation that Leontes spreads at his court, and a spring and summer half, centring on the mutual love of Florizel and Perdita and the reunions at the end. Like Macbeth, Leontes creates a wintry landscape of death and desolation around him, destroying all happiness and good fellowship. But whereas Macbeth, the winter-king, has to be killed before spring and new life – embodied by Malcolm – can reign in Scotland, Leontes is made to undergo a long process of purgation. This too is a desolate and wintry period, as is vividly suggested by Paulina's description of the necessary penance:

> *A thousand knees,*
> *Ten thousand years together, naked, fasting,*
> *Upon a barren mountain, and still winter*
> *In storm perpetual, could not move the gods*
> *To look that way thou wert.* III.2.208–12

But this desolate period comes to an end with the arrival at his court of Florizel and Perdita, whom he greets with the words:

> *Welcome hither*
> *As is the spring to th'earth!* V.1.150–51

The scene of the sheep-shearing feast is used by Shakespeare to present those human values which Leontes had banished from his court: love, joy, hospitality, good fellowship. While the time of the year is midsummer, when bright Phoebus is in his strength and 'great creating Nature', the goddess presiding over this part of the play, reigns supreme, some of the most memorable allusions are to spring, the spring embodied by the young lovers. There is Florizel's description of Perdita as

> *no shepherdess, but Flora*
> *Peering in April's front;* IV.4.2–3

there is Perdita's great speech about spring flowers (IV.4.112–29); and there is Autolycus's opening song,

When daffodils begin to peer,
With heigh, the doxy over the dale,
Why, then comes in the sweet o'the year,
For the red blood reigns in the winter's pale.

IV.3.1–4

'For the red blood reigns in the winter's pale'. .... The
line sums up the basic progression of the play.

Between the two contrasting halves Shakespeare introduced a transitional scene at the end of the destructive
phase. In this scene, which depicts the death of Antigonus
and the mariners at the very moment of the Shepherd's
discovery of the babe, we pass from horror to comedy,
indeed see horror turned into comedy by the way in
which the Clown is made to report the double calamity.
The transition is summed up by the Shepherd's words to
his son: 'Now bless thyself: thou met'st with things dying,
I with things new-born' (III.3.109–10).

But the relation between the two halves of the play
consists not only of a series of contrasts but also of a series
of parallels. At the beginning of each half stands a brief
prose scene of about the same length, consisting of a
dialogue between Camillo and another person. In each the
conversation partly turns upon a happy and harmonious
relation, which is soon to be violently disturbed: that
between Polixenes and Leontes in the first half and that
between their children, Florizel and Perdita, in the second.
In each half Shakespeare then proceeds to bring before us
this relation as it exists before its disturbance. Next, in the
brief dialogue between Leontes and Hermione (I.2.88–105)
Shakespeare conveys the joyful and loving communion
that exists between them at the play's opening. In the
same way the close and loving relation between Leontes
and Mamillius (I.2.151–72) and, finally, between Her-

mione and Mamillius (II.1.1–32) is presented to us. Shakespeare is evidently at pains to establish clearly at the outset all that Leontes loses and destroys.

In a similar way in the play's second half the joyful and loving relation between Florizel and Perdita is fully brought out before its would-be destroyer, Polixenes, unmasks himself. The effect, as in the first half, is that of the sudden and violent intrusion of winter, blasting the blossoms of spring. Already, earlier in this scene, Shakespeare has made Perdita give flowers of winter to Polixenes (IV.4.73–9), and has made him swear 'By my white beard' (IV.4.401). Whatever the *moral* differences, the imaginative impact of the cruel threats of Polixenes is very similar to that of the ravings of Leontes. We need only compare the words of Leontes to Antigonus,

> *Thou, traitor, hast set on thy wife to this.*
> *My child? Away with't! Even thou, that hast*
> *A heart so tender o'er it, take it hence*
> *And see it instantly consumed with fire:*
> *Even thou, and none but thou. Take it up straight!*
> *Within this hour bring me word 'tis done,*
> *And by good testimony, or I'll seize thy life,*
> *With what thou else call'st thine. If thou refuse,*
> *And wilt encounter with my wrath, say so:*
> *The bastard brains with these my proper hands*
> *Shall I dash out ...*   II.3.130–40

with the threats of Polixenes to the old Shepherd and Perdita:

>   *Thou, old traitor,*
> *I am sorry that by hanging thee I can*
> *But shorten thy life one week. – And thou, fresh piece*
> *Of excellent witchcraft, who of force must know*
> *The royal fool thou cop'st with ...*

> *I'll have thy beauty scratched with briers and made*
> *More homely than thy state. . . .*
>   *if ever henceforth thou*
> *These rural latches to his entrance open,*
> *Or hoop his body more with thy embraces,*
> *I will devise a death as cruel for thee*
> *As thou art tender to't.*   IV.4.417–23, 434–8

Autolycus gives what amounts to a *reductio ad absurdum* of this outburst in his talk with the Clown later in the scene:

> *He has a son : who shall be flayed alive ; then, 'nointed over*
> *with honey, set on the head of a wasp's nest ; then stand till*
> *he be three-quarters and a dram dead; then recovered*
> *again with aqua-vitae or some other hot infusion; then,*
> *raw as he is, and in the hottest day prognostication pro-*
> *claims, shall he be set against a brick wall, the sun looking*
> *with a southward eye upon him, where he is to behold him*
> *with flies blown to death.*   IV.4.779–87

It takes our mind back to Paulina's outcry in the first half of the play:

> *What studied torments, tyrant, hast for me ?*
> *What wheels ? Racks ? Fires ? What flaying ? Boiling*
> *In leads or oils ?*   III.2.173–5

The effect of the tyrannical behaviour of Polixenes is that Perdita is for a second time committed to the mercy of the waves, as she flees with Florizel to Sicilia. In both halves Camillo plays the same role, counselling the victim of the King's anger and helping him to escape from the realm to a place of safety – a parallel which is made explicit when Florizel calls him 'Preserver of my father, now of me' (IV.4.583).

34

At the end of each half stands the scene which provides its climax: the trial-scene in the first half, the statue-scene in the second. In each our attention centres on Hermione: Hermione pleading eloquently in her own defence in the trial-scene; Hermione standing silent and motionless before us in the statue-scene. The first half culminates in her death, the second in her 'resurrection'. Structural parallel and thematic contrast are here combined.

Our sense of the similarity, the repetition in the two halves of the play, which we experience despite our awareness of the predominant contrasts between them, is accentuated by the Chorus-speech of Time, which separates them and comes almost exactly in the middle of the play. After a playful defence of the poet's violation of the unity of time in *The Winter's Tale*,

> *since it is in my power*
> *To o'erthrow law, and in one self-born hour*
> *To plant and o'erwhelm custom*

Time declares:

> *Your patience this allowing,*
> *I turn my glass, and give my scene such growing*
> *As you had slept between.*   IV.1.15–17

By his gesture of turning the hour-glass Time marks the great break between the two halves of the play, but also creates in us a feeling that the action is starting all over again. Both parts of the hour-glass look alike, and it may not be fanciful to think that this fact enhances our sense of the similarity of the shape and structure of the two halves of *The Winter's Tale*.

That sense is also enhanced by its imagery. More than any other of Shakespeare's plays, it resembles *Macbeth* in

the nature and use of its imagery, a kinship which derives
from an affinity of themes. This is above all true of the first
half, which shares with *Macbeth* the contrast of images of
planting and growth with those of uprooting and blight,
and of images of health and physic with those of sickness
and infection. In the opening scene the positives in both
groups of images are introduced. Of the friendship of
Leontes and Polixenes we are told that 'there rooted
betwixt them then such an affection, which cannot choose
but branch now' (I.1.23-4), while Mamillius is declared
to be 'one that indeed physics the subject, makes old
hearts fresh' (I.1.37-8). And in the following scene
Polixenes says of his son:

> *He makes a July's day short as December,*
> *And with his varying childness cures in me*
> *Thoughts that would thick my blood.* I.2.169-71

In *Macbeth* it is the English king who is represented as a
source of healing, in opposition to Macbeth, the source of
infection and disease. In *The Winter's Tale* it is, significantly, above all the young who fill this role, in contrast
to Leontes, in whose ravings disease-images abound.

Great creating Nature, *natura naturans*, who presides
over the scene of the sheep-shearing feast, is also twice
referred to in the first half of the play, each time by
Paulina, and each time in connexion with the birth of
Perdita (II.2.60 and II.3.103). For the birth of Perdita
fills a role in the first half of the play similar to that of her
love for Florizel in the second half, setting the creative,
fertile, and natural against the destructive, barren, and
monstrous.

Imagery drawn from nature is found repeatedly in the
first half of the play. Its second scene opens with the words
of Polixenes,

Nine changes of the watery star hath been
The shepherd's note since we have left our throne
Without a burden.

And a little later in the scene he compares his boyhood
friendship with Leontes to

twinned lambs that did frisk i'th'sun,
And bleat the one at th'other.   I.2.67–8

What are here poetic embroideries or figures of speech
are introduced into the second part on a more literal level:
we meet real shepherds, who talk of real sheep, just as the
images of planting and growing, used purely figuratively in
the first half, reappear in the second half on a more literal
level in the horticultural debate between Polixenes and
Perdita and in the flowers she distributes. But their
symbolic suggestiveness in both halves is basically the
same.

Even in their imagery, then, the two halves are linked in
a variety of ways. And just as the scene of the sheep-
shearing feast, with its images of spring, of fertility,
and growth, has its corresponding images in the first half
of the play, the statue-scene has its equivalent in the
'ceremonious, solemn, and unearthly' atmosphere of the
Delphic oracle, as described by Cleomenes and Dion in
III.1.

We have seen, then, that the structural pattern of *The
Winter's Tale* consists not only of a series of contrasts
between its two halves but also of a series of parallels.
Yet whereas the contrasts are clearly instrumental in con-
veying the play's 'meaning', the function of the parallels is
far less obvious. Though *The Winter's Tale* is full of
dramatic irony – as is not surprising in a play concerned so
much with human blindness and ignorance – the parallels,
like the contrasts, are not, for the most part, of an ironic

nature. In *Coriolanus*, another play divided into two sharply contrasted halves, with a pattern of repetition in the action, the pervasive parallels and contrasts between the incidents of the two halves are filled with dramatic irony, an irony which is, indeed, a central effect of the play and a chief vehicle of its significance. There is nothing of this in the parallels and contrasts of *The Winter's Tale*. Only in Camillo's role as preserver of Florizel from the wrath of Polixenes, the very person whom he had previously preserved from the wrath of Leontes, can an element of dramatic irony be discerned.

Perhaps we come a little closer to an understanding of the significance of the parallels between the two halves of *The Winter's Tale* if we compare them with those between the two parts of *Pericles*. The sudden and violent blows of fortune that strike Marina, as they had earlier struck her father, deepen and widen the play's image of life as a lasting storm, whirring us from our friends. In a similar way the principal effect of the pattern of repetition in *The Winter's Tale* is to increase our sense of the fragility, the precariousness of human happiness. As we watch, twice over in the play's events, the progression from summer to winter, with the return of spring and summer in the end, the affinity between human affairs and the cycle of the seasons is borne in upon us.

*

There are two main characteristics which mark off Shakespeare's Last Plays from his previous comedies. One is the intrusion of the supernatural, which does not enter the earlier comedies, with the single exception of *A Midsummer Night's Dream*. It comes into *Pericles* in the form of the goddess Diana, who appears to the hero in a vision; into *Cymbeline* through Jupiter, who descends on his eagle and prophesies; into *The Tempest* through Ariel and his fellow-spirits. In *The Winter's Tale* it does not take visible shape, but plays a crucial part through the oracle of Apollo. But this remains its only intervention in the play. Commentators have often extended its role by speaking of Apollo inducing the death of Mamillius as a punishment for his father's blasphemy. This is how it appears to Leontes at the time, dazed under the blow (III.2.144–5), but the audience is assuredly not meant to share this belief. Had Shakespeare wished it to do so, he would not have made the servant bring the news of the boy's death only a moment after Leontes utters his blasphemy. Above all he would not have provided a natural explanation for it, first by references to Mamillius's illness (II.3.10–17) and then by making both the servant (III.2.142–3) and Paulina (III.2.193–6) declare that he died from a broken heart because of the treatment suffered by his mother.

In *Pandosto* Fortune is the presiding divinity, made responsible for most of its events. Her name is for ever on the lips of both the narrator and his characters. She plays not only her traditional roles, such as that of providing storms and favourable winds at sea, but also, very strangely, usurps those of other divinities by, for instance, lending Pandosto and his queen a son, or making Dorastus and Fawnia fall in love with each other. The gods are rarely mentioned as controllers of human destiny. Shakespeare did not share Greene's obsession with Fortune. He reduced her role in the plot by making it seem human purpose, not accident, that brings the infant Perdita to Bohemia (III.3.1–2 and 30–31 are probably meant to suggest that Antigonus takes her there in fulfilment of Hermione's command in his dream-vision); and again by making it human purpose, not accident, that brings Florizel and Perdita to the court of Leontes. And she is seldom directly referred to in the course of *The Winter's Tale*. Shakespeare allows Fortune her place in the events of the play (for instance, in making all the mariners and Antigonus die) but it is a very subordinate place. Yet this does not mean that instead of Fortune he shows Providence or the gods to be in control of the events, as has sometimes been claimed. Nowhere in the play is there any suggestion of this. There are not even the attributions of its happenings to a higher power which are usually made by Shakespeare's virtuous characters. It is man's wishes, fears, and imaginings, rather than Fortune, Providence, or the gods, which are depicted as the prime movers of the play's events.

The other main characteristic which marks off Shakespeare's Last Plays from his previous comedies is the much greater weight and scope given to the scenes depicting the reunion with loved relatives believed to be dead (here the only exception among earlier comedies is *Twelfth Night*). In three of the four Last Plays this reunion is accompanied by reconciliation and forgiveness, the exception being *Pericles*, in which the reunited parties have nothing to forgive each other. In discussions of these plays it is often remarked that it is the mutual love of the children which brings about the reconciliation of the parents. It is an odd claim, for it does not hold true of a single one of them. There *is* a play of Shakespeare's of which it holds true, but it is an early tragedy, *Romeo and Juliet*. And it also holds true of *Pandosto*, where the two kings remain, strangely, unreconciled, so that even sixteen years after the tragic events of the first part Egistus, we are told, 'hated no man so much as Pandosto'. Here it really *is* the love of the children which leads to the reconciliation of their fathers and hence of the two kingdoms, so that the ambassadors of Egistus 'rejoiced that their young prince had made such a choice, that those kingdoms, which through enmity had long time been dissevered, should now through perpetual amity be united and reconciled'. In *The Winter's Tale* Shakespeare paints a very different picture. When the second part of the play opens, the two kings are reunited in friendship, so that Polixenes can speak of Leontes as 'that penitent ... and reconciled king, my brother' (IV.2.21–3), and Camillo can advise Florizel to take refuge at the court of Leontes because of the loving reception of which he is there assured. Far from being instrumental in reconciling the two kings, Florizel has to ask the help of Leontes in reconciling him with his father. Rather than agents of reconciliation, the young in *The Winter's Tale* are, above all, emblems of the state of innocence which their elders have lost (see I.2.67–75).

*

Much of the criticism of *The Winter's Tale*, especially in the last thirty years, has been concerned with the search for deeper significances, the unveiling of an 'inner meaning' hidden below the surface of the play. We may conveniently divide criticism of this kind into four main groups.

The first consists of critics who perceive a specifically Christian meaning in the play. Their interpretations range from the discovery of full-fledged allegory to that of intermittent symbolism. The Christian article of faith most commonly seen as receiving symbolic expression in the play is that of man's resurrection and reunion with loved relatives in Heaven, as conveyed through the statue-scene. But if this is really what the scene is supposed to suggest, it seems very odd that there should be an emphasis on Hermione's having grown wrinkled, on her looking sixteen years older than when she was last seen. The least we can demand of any interpretation is that it should not make Shakespeare appear as someone who has bungled his job.

Readers may feel that another of the Christian interpretations (for they are mutually exclusive) fits the facts better. Nevill Coghill remarks that

'The spiritual meaning of the play in no way depends on [Hermione] being a Lazarus or an Alcestis. It is a play about a crisis in the life of Leontes, not of Hermione, and her restoration to him (it is not a "resurrection") is something which happens not to her, but to *him*. He had thought her dead by his own hand ("She I kill'd") and now finds her unexpectedly alive in the guardianship of Paulina. (So a man who believed himself to have destroyed his soul by some great sin might, after a long repentance under his Conscience, find that that very Conscience had unknown to him kept his soul in being and could at last restore it to him alive and whole.)'

(*Shakespeare Survey 11*, page 40)

But this reading entails an excessive concentration upon Leontes and impoverishes the statue-scene by encouraging us to neglect an element which is clearly of great importance in it: the reunion of mother and daughter.

The second group of critics links *The Winter's Tale* with vegetation-myths, and especially with that of Ceres and Proserpina. Perdita, like Proserpina, is separated from her mother and later reunited with her, and is emblematic of spring. But here the resemblance ends, and the two stories are utterly different: in the one we have the abduction of a young woman by Pluto, and her mother's search for her through the world; in the other the exposure of an infant, her upbringing by a shepherd, and her mother's self-sequestration for sixteen years. The importance of the symbolism of the cycle of the seasons throughout the play is evident. But there is no warrant for finding a specific myth shadowed in its events.

Where the first two groups of critics discover the play's 'inner meaning' in symbolic significances below the surface of *The Winter's Tale*, the last two find it in underlying themes. One of these themes, which has been much emphasized, is that of the relation of court and country. Shakespeare, we are told, implies the need for an intermarriage of the sober virtues of the country with the graces of the court. In Perdita, who is of royal birth but of country nurture, is seen an emblem of such happy intermarriage.

There are plays by Shakespeare in which the relative merits of the life of court and country are much discussed, notably *As You Like It* and *Cymbeline*. In *Pandosto*, too, Fawnia is made to deliver a set speech on the subject. In *The Winter's Tale* it is nowhere explicitly mentioned. Neither are there any signs of its being raised implicitly. Perdita is in no way presented as an exemplar of rustic virtues. What is emphasized again and again is the fact that she is so utterly different from what her country upbringing would lead one to expect, that, as Polixenes puts it,

> *nothing she does or seems*
> *But smacks of something greater than herself,*
> *Too noble for this place.*   IV.4.157–9

That in spite of her rustic nurture she has not become another Mopsa and Dorcas is due to her princely nature, which shows itself in all she says and does. The theme of nature asserting itself in spite of nurture is common in romance and had been given much prominence by Shakespeare in *Cymbeline*, where it is exemplified in the two young princes, whose royal nature constantly manifests itself, in spite of their upbringing in a mountain-cave. Shakespeare would hardly show Perdita to be a paragon both *in spite of* her country nurture and *because* she combined the virtues of the country with those of the court. The rustic virtues are exemplified by the old Shepherd. But nowhere in the play is there any suggestion that these ought to be married with those of the court. Neither the court of Leontes nor that of Polixenes (of which we scarcely get a glimpse) is shown to be in need of regeneration. On the contrary, Shakespeare emphasizes the integrity and probity of the Sicilian courtiers, their freedom from servility, their refusal to echo the King's moods and to share his delusions.

Where the third group of critics finds a dominant theme in the play's concern with the relation of court and country, the fourth group finds it in the kindred concern with the relation of Art and Nature. It is first raised in the great debate between Perdita and Polixenes about the use of art in gardening (IV.4.86–103); and it returns in another form in the last Act, when the artist who created the statue is praised for being Nature's ape (V.2.95–8), while, in the final scene, when the statue proves to be alive, 'great creating Nature' is vindicated as the supreme artist.

The arguments advanced by Polixenes in favour of cross-breeding in gardening – which the third group of critics interpret as Shakespeare's implicit advocacy of the intermarriage of rustic virtues and courtly graces – were a Renaissance commonplace, ultimately going back to Aristotle. And Perdita's primitivist position, echoing Montaigne (see Commentary on IV.4.86–103), was equally familiar. The dramatic irony of the debate, in which both speakers are apparently oblivious of its relevance to the intended marriage of the young lovers, sufficiently justifies its prominent position in the scene. There is nothing profound or original in the debate, no philosophic truths relevant to the rest of the play are being unveiled. Neither has the mention of Nature and Art in the last Act – where the relation is one not of *improving* Nature through Art but of perfectly *imitating* her – anything but local significance. We do well to remember Philip Edwards's admonition: 'It is a disservice to Shakespeare to pretend that one is adding to his profundity by discovering that his plots are symbolic vehicles for ideas and perceptions which are, for the most part, banal, trite, and colourless' (*Shakespeare Survey 11*, page 11).

Of the many, complex reasons for the search for an 'inner meaning' in the criticism of *The Winter's Tale*, two stand out most clearly. One is the wish to receive from Shakespeare, in what may be his last play written without a collaborator, if not some message on how we ought to live, at least some profound vision of man's existence on earth. The simple suggestion that human happiness is precarious, that barren winter may follow suddenly upon the rich joys of spring and summer, which is expressed through the action of the play, does not meet this demand, and the search for further, deeper significances is therefore pursued. The other reason seems to be a dissatisfaction with the play, its seemingly sprawling nature, its apparent lack of cohesion, the absurdity or incredibility of some of its events. Hence the desire to give coherence and unity to it by discovering some 'inner meaning' which will make everything fall into place.

There are signs in the criticism of recent years that this dissatisfaction is yielding to a juster appreciation of the play's greatness. Its construction is coming to be seen not as clumsy and artless but as entirely purposeful and carefully planned, the proper vehicle for the play's significances; the seeming absurdities or improbabilities of its plot are perceived to be in keeping with the *genre* of dramatic romance to which it belongs, and the effect upon the audience which it is designed to produce. Coleridge called *The Winter's Tale* 'this delightful drama', and a recent critic speaks of it as 'Shakespeare's most beautiful play'. Its intensely moving events, the rich variety of its characters and incidents, and, above all, the splendour of its language, put it among his most masterly creations.

FURTHER READING

The most comprehensively edited text of the play so far is J. H. P. Pafford's Arden edition (1963), though Stephen Orgel's Oxford Shakespeare edition is to appear in 1996. Like most other editors, Pafford believes the composition of the play to follow *Pericles* and *Cymbeline* and to precede *The Tempest*. The Oxford Shakespeare *Complete Works* (1986) places the play before *Cymbeline*, perhaps in 1609–10. Whatever the precise order of composition, most commentators agree that *The Winter's Tale* is intimately connected in theme and mood with the other three Romances and treat it accordingly. Perhaps the most important book dealing with the last plays as a group is Howard Felperin's *Shakespearean Romance* (1972). In examining the major developments behind Shakespeare's appropriation of romance, Felperin highlights the distinctiveness of Shakespeare's contribution – how his Romances constitute a vale of soulmaking in which loss, brutality, humiliation, ageing (Hermione's wrinkles) are the necessary prelude to the experience of grace, faith, atonement, miracle. This salutary, Shakespearean conjunction is the topic of much interesting work on these plays. Charles Frey's *Shakespeare's Vast Romance, a Study of 'The Winter's Tale'* (1980) and his essay, ' "O sacred, shadowy, cold, and constant queen": Shakespeare's Imperiled and Chastening Daughters of Romance' in *The Woman's Part: Feminist Criticism of Shakespeare* (1980) turn on the proposition that, despite the plays' gifts of redemption, they 'may be more patriarchal and patrilineal in perspective than Shakespearean interpreters have yet cared or dared to recognize'. A. D. Nuttall's *William Shakespeare: 'The Winter's Tale'* (1966), in a scene-by-scene analysis, pursues the play's double vision, as does Bill Overton in his work on the play in the Critics Debate series (1989) and Barbara A. Mowat in *The Dramaturgy of Shakespeare's Romances* (1976). Boika Sokolova's *Shakespeare's Romances as Interrogative Texts: Their Alienation Strategies and Ideology* (1992) makes much of the relevance of Brecht to that double vision and much too, as do Frey and others, of the male characters' ruinous patriarchal behaviour.

Ruinous patriarchal behaviour doesn't square with another traditional line of enquiry which emphasizes the plays' beneficent providence. This frequently takes a specifically Christian – and hence also patriarchal – form, as in S. L. Bethell's *The Winter's Tale: A Study* (1947), which talks of the play in terms of a Christianity 'newly translated into terms of the romance'. Richard Pilgrim's *You Precious Winners All: A Study of 'The Winter's Tale'* (1983) believes the play follows 'the essential character of the doctrine of the body of Christ'. Cynthia Marshall's *Last Things and Last Plays: Shakespearean Eschatology* (1991) more provocatively explores the disjunctions between the workings of belief in the theatre and the real world. The image of Hermione's 'resurrection', she says, 'offers a kind of imaginative fulfillment but offers nothing to believe in but the power of the theater'.

Many other works explore this theme in less restricted metaphysical terms. Northrop Frye's *A Natural Perspective: The Development of Shakespearean Comedy and Romance* (1955) pursues it in terms of mythic descent in which the plays satisfy our deepest longings. R. G. Hunter's *Shakespeare and the Comedy of Forgiveness* (1965), Marco Mincoff's *Things Supernatural and Causeless: Shakespearean Romance* (1992) and D. L. Peterson's *Time, Tide and Tempest: A Study of Shakespeare's Romances* (1973) all emphasize the benignity, however perplexingly evolved, of the final vision. Gary Schmidgall's *Shakespeare and the Courtly Aesthetic* (1981) insists that the Last Plays celebrate an 'astonishing recovery of political optimism'; David Bergeron's *Shakespeare's Romances and the Royal Family* (1985) celebrates

Shakespeare's celebration of family love; D. W. Harding's 'Shakespeare's Final View of Women', *TLS*, 30 November (1979) says that the final view of women is a restorative one (except in the case of Dionyza and Cymbeline's Queen); R. S. White's *'Let wonder seem familiar': Endings in Shakespeare's Romance Vision* (1985), like Frye's work, concludes that the Romances teach us that 'by seeing the best, by wishing for the best, we may create the best'. H. W. Fawkner's *Shakespeare's Miracle Plays* (1992) looks at *Pericles*, *Cymbeline*, and *The Winter's Tale* as 'miracle' plays and gives us a 'hyperontological analysis of miracle' in *The Winter's Tale*.

The Winter's Tale attracts many critics with its linguistic bravura. In *Drama Within Drama: Shakespeare's Sense of His Art in 'King Lear', 'The Winter's Tale' and 'The Tempest'* (1972), Robert Egan talks of the play as an 'aggressive artistic manifesto'. Maurice Hunt's *Shakespeare's Romance of the Word* (1990) claims that in this play Shakespeare continues to 'dramatize problems intrinsic to speech as a communicative medium'. Ruth Nevo's *Shakespeare's Other Language* (1987) argues that Shakespeare's drama is wilder than we think, and that *The Winter's Tale* 'is a *tour de force* in the theatre of reverie'. A little more on the conventional side are Hallett Smith's *Shakespeare's Romances: A Study of Some Ways of the Imagination* (1972) and R. W. Uphaus's *Beyond Tragedy: Structure and Experiment in Shakespeare's Romances* (1981). A little too conventional, perhaps, are Robert M. Adams's *Shakespeare: The Four Romances* (1989), Elizabeth Bieman's *William Shakespeare: The Romances* (1984), Fitzroy Pyle's *'The Winter's Tale': A Commentary on the Structure* (1968), and Wilbur Sanders in a Harvester New Critical Introduction (1987).

An exhaustive account of the play on the stage is given by Dennis Bartholomeusz in *'The Winter's Tale' in Performance in England and America, 1611–1976* (1982) and David A. Male in *Shakespeare on Stage: 'The Winter's Tale'* (1984). The Arden edition has an extended essay on the subject. R. P. Draper focuses on a number of productions in his volume in the Text and Performance Series (1985).

THE CHARACTERS IN THE PLAY

LEONTES, King of Sicilia
HERMIONE, his wife
MAMILLIUS, his son
PERDITA, his daughter
CAMILLO
ANTIGONUS
CLEOMENES } Lords at the court of Leontes
DION
PAULINA, wife of Antigonus
EMILIA, a lady attending on Hermione
A Gaoler
A Mariner
Other Lords and Gentlemen, Ladies, Officers, and
    Servants at the court of Leontes

POLIXENES, King of Bohemia
FLORIZEL, his son
ARCHIDAMUS, a Bohemian Lord
AUTOLYCUS, a rogue
Old SHEPHERD, reputed father of Perdita
CLOWN, his son
MOPSA } shepherdesses
DORCAS
A Servant of the old Shepherd
Other Shepherds and Shepherdesses
Twelve countrymen disguised as satyrs

TIME, as Chorus

ARCHIDAMUS If you shall chance, Camillo, to visit Bohemia, on the like occasion whereon my services are now
on foot, you shall see, as I have said, great difference betwixt our Bohemia and your Sicilia.

CAMILLO I think this coming summer the King of Sicilia
means to pay Bohemia the visitation which he justly
owes him.

ARCHIDAMUS Wherein our entertainment shall shame
us: we will be justified in our loves. For indeed –

CAMILLO Beseech you –   10

ARCHIDAMUS Verily, I speak it in the freedom of my
knowledge: we cannot with such magnificence, in so
rare – I know not what to say. We will give you sleepy
drinks, that your senses, unintelligent of our insuf-
ficience, may, though they cannot praise us, as little
accuse us.

CAMILLO You pay a great deal too dear for what's given
freely.

ARCHIDAMUS Believe me, I speak as my understanding
instructs me and as mine honesty puts it to utterance.   20

CAMILLO Sicilia cannot show himself over-kind to Bohemia. They were trained together in their childhoods;
and there rooted betwixt them then such an affection,
which cannot choose but branch now. Since their more
mature dignities and royal necessities made separation
of their society, their encounters, though not personal,
hath been royally attorneyed with interchange of gifts,

53

letters, loving embassies: that they have seemed to be
together, though absent; shook hands as over a vast;
30 and embraced, as it were, from the ends of opposed
winds. The heavens continue their loves!

ARCHIDAMUS I think there is not in the world either
malice or matter to alter it. You have an unspeakable
comfort of your young prince Mamillius. It is a gentleman of the greatest promise that ever came into my note.

CAMILLO I very well agree with you in the hopes of him.
It is a gallant child; one that indeed physics the subject,
makes old hearts fresh. They that went on crutches ere
he was born desire yet their life to see him a man.

40 ARCHIDAMUS Would they else be content to die?

CAMILLO Yes – if there were no other excuse why they
should desire to live.

ARCHIDAMUS If the King had no son, they would desire
to live on crutches till he had one.   *Exeunt*

I.2   *Enter Leontes, Hermione, Mamillius, Polixenes,
             Camillo, and Attendants*

POLIXENES
Nine changes of the watery star hath been
The shepherd's note since we have left our throne
Without a burden. Time as long again
Would be filled up, my brother, with our thanks,
And yet we should for perpetuity
Go hence in debt. And therefore, like a cipher
Yet standing in rich place, I multiply
With one 'We thank you' many thousands more
That go before it.

LEONTES   Stay your thanks a while,
10 And pay them when you part.

POLIXENES   Sir, that's tomorrow.

54

I am questioned by my fears of what may chance
Or breed upon our absence. That may blow
No sneaping winds at home, to make us say
'This is put forth too truly'! Besides, I have stayed
To tire your royalty.

LEONTES   We are tougher, brother,
Than you can put us to't.

POLIXENES   No longer stay.

LEONTES
One sev'n-night longer.

POLIXENES   Very sooth, tomorrow.

LEONTES
We'll part the time between's then; and in that
I'll no gainsaying.

POLIXENES   Press me not, beseech you, so.
There is no tongue that moves, none, none i'th'world,   20
So soon as yours could win me. So it should now,
Were there necessity in your request, although
'Twere needful I denied it. My affairs
Do even drag me homeward; which to hinder
Were, in your love, a whip to me, my stay
To you a charge and trouble. To save both,
Farewell, our brother.

LEONTES   Tongue-tied, our queen? Speak you.

HERMIONE
I had thought, sir, to have held my peace until
You had drawn oaths from him not to stay. You, sir,
Charge him too coldly. Tell him you are sure   30
All in Bohemia's well: this satisfaction
The by-gone day proclaimed. Say this to him,
He's beat from his best ward.

LEONTES   Well said, Hermione.

HERMIONE
To tell he longs to see his son were strong.

55

But let him say so, then, and let him go;
But let him swear so and he shall not stay:
We'll thwack him hence with distaffs.

Leontes draws apart

Yet of your royal presence I'll adventure
The borrow of a week. When at Bohemia
40 You take my lord, I'll give him my commission
To let him there a month behind the gest
Prefixed for's parting; yet, good deed, Leontes,
I love thee not a jar o'th'clock behind
What lady she her lord. You'll stay?

POLIXENES   No, madam.

HERMIONE
Nay, but you will!

POLIXENES   I may not, verily.

HERMIONE
Verily!
You put me off with limber vows; but I,
Though you would seek t'unsphere the stars with oaths,
Should yet say, 'Sir, no going'. Verily,
50 You shall not go. A lady's 'verily' is
As potent as a lord's. Will you go yet?
Force me to keep you as a prisoner,
Not like a guest; so you shall pay your fees
When you depart, and save your thanks. How say you?
My prisoner? Or my guest? By your dread 'verily',
One of them you shall be.

POLIXENES   Your guest, then, madam:
To be your prisoner should import offending;
Which is for me less easy to commit
Than you to punish.

HERMIONE   Not your gaoler, then,
60 But your kind hostess. Come, I'll question you
Of my lord's tricks, and yours, when you were boys.

56

You were pretty lordings then?
POLIXENES   We were, fair Queen,
Two lads that thought there was no more behind
But such a day tomorrow as today,
And to be boy eternal.
HERMIONE   Was not my lord
The verier wag o'th'two?
POLIXENES
We were as twinned lambs that did frisk i'th'sun,
And bleat the one at th'other. What we changed
Was innocence for innocence: we knew not
The doctrine of ill-doing, nor dreamed   70
That any did. Had we pursued that life,
And our weak spirits ne'er been higher reared
With stronger blood, we should have answered heaven
Boldly 'Not guilty', the imposition cleared
Hereditary ours.
HERMIONE   By this we gather
You have tripped since.
POLIXENES   O my most sacred lady,
Temptations have since then been born to's: for
In those unfledged days was my wife a girl;
Your precious self had then not crossed the eyes
Of my young playfellow.
HERMIONE   Grace to boot!   80
Of this make no conclusion, lest you say
Your queen and I are devils. Yet go on:
Th'offences we have made you do we'll answer,
If you first sinned with us, and that with us
You did continue fault, and that you slipped not
With any but with us.
LEONTES (approaching) Is he won yet?
HERMIONE
He'll stay, my lord.

LEONTES   At my request he would not.
Hermione, my dearest, thou never spok'st
To better purpose.

HERMIONE   Never?

LEONTES   Never but once.

HERMIONE

90   What? Have I twice said well? When was't before?
I prithee tell me. Cram's with praise, and make's
As fat as tame things. One good deed dying tongueless
Slaughters a thousand waiting upon that.
Our praises are our wages. You may ride's
With one soft kiss a thousand furlongs ere
With spur we heat an acre. But to th'goal:
My last good deed was to entreat his stay.
What was my first? It has an elder sister,
Or I mistake you. O, would her name were Grace!
100 But once before I spoke to th'purpose? When?
Nay, let me have't; I long.

LEONTES   Why, that was when
Three crabbèd months had soured themselves to death
Ere I could make thee open thy white hand
And clap thyself my love: then didst thou utter
'I am yours for ever'.

HERMIONE   'Tis Grace indeed.
Why, lo you now, I have spoke to th'purpose twice:
The one for ever earned a royal husband;
Th'other for some while a friend.

She gives her hand to Polixenes

LEONTES (*aside*)   Too hot, too hot!
To mingle friendship far is mingling bloods.
110 I have *tremor cordis* on me: my heart dances,
But not for joy, not joy. This entertainment
May a free face put on, derive a liberty
From heartiness, from bounty, fertile bosom,

58

And well become the agent – 't may, I grant.
But to be paddling palms and pinching fingers,
As now they are, and making practised smiles
As in a looking glass; and then to sigh, as 'twere
The mort o'th'deer – O, that is entertainment
My bosom likes not, nor my brows! Mamillius,
Art thou my boy?

MAMILLIUS   Ay, my good lord.

LEONTES   I'fecks!   120
Why, that's my bawcock. What, hast smutched thy
          nose?
They say it is a copy out of mine. Come, captain,
We must be neat – not neat but cleanly, captain.
And yet the steer, the heifer, and the calf
Are all called neat. Still virginalling
Upon his palm? – How now, you wanton calf!
Art thou my calf?

MAMILLIUS   Yes, if you will, my lord.

LEONTES
Thou want'st a rough pash and the shoots that I have
To be full like me; yet they say we are
Almost as like as eggs. Women say so,   130
That will say anything. But were they false
As o'er-dyed blacks, as wind, as waters, false
As dice are to be wished by one that fixes
No bourn 'twixt his and mine, yet were it true
To say this boy were like me. Come, sir page,
Look on me with your welkin eye. Sweet villain!
Most dear'st! My collop! Can thy dam? May't be?
Affection, thy intention stabs the centre.
Thou dost make possible things not so held,
Communicat'st with dreams – how can this be? –   140
With what's unreal thou coactive art,
And fellow'st nothing. Then 'tis very credent

59

Thou mayst co-join with something; and thou dost,
And that beyond commission, and I find it,
And that to the infection of my brains
And hardening of my brows.

POLIXENES   What means Sicilia?

HERMIONE
He something seems unsettled.

POLIXENES   How, my lord!
What cheer? How is't with you, best brother?

HERMIONE   You look
As if you held a brow of much distraction.
150   Are you moved, my lord?

LEONTES   No, in good earnest.
How sometimes Nature will betray its folly,
Its tenderness, and make itself a pastime
To harder bosoms! Looking on the lines
Of my boy's face, methoughts I did recoil
Twenty-three years, and saw myself unbreeched,
In my green velvet coat; my dagger muzzled,
Lest it should bite its master and so prove,
As ornaments oft does, too dangerous.
How like, methought, I then was to this kernel,
160   This squash, this gentleman. Mine honest friend,
Will you take eggs for money?

MAMILLIUS
No, my lord, I'll fight.

LEONTES
You will? Why, happy man be's dole! My brother,
Are you so fond of your young prince as we
Do seem to be of ours?

POLIXENES   If at home, sir,
He's all my exercise, my mirth, my matter;
Now my sworn friend, and then mine enemy;
My parasite, my soldier, statesman, all.

He makes a July's day short as December,
And with his varying childness cures in me   170
Thoughts that would thick my blood.

LEONTES   So stands this squire
Officed with me. We two will walk, my lord,
And leave you to your graver steps. Hermione,
How thou lov'st us show in our brother's welcome.
Let what is dear in Sicily be cheap.
Next to thyself and my young rover, he's
Apparent to my heart.

HERMIONE   If you would seek us,
We are yours i'th'garden. Shall's attend you there?

LEONTES
To your own bents dispose you: you'll be found,
Be you beneath the sky. (*Aside*) I am angling now,   180
Though you perceive me not how I give line.
Go to, go to!
How she holds up the neb, the bill to him!
And arms her with the boldness of a wife
To her allowing husband!

                              Exeunt Hermione and Polixenes
                              Gone already!
Inch-thick, knee-deep, o'er head and ears a forked one!
Go play, boy, play: thy mother plays, and I
Play too – but so disgraced a part, whose issue
Will hiss me to my grave. Contempt and clamour
Will be my knell. Go play, boy, play. There have been, 190
Or I am much deceived, cuckolds ere now;
And many a man there is, even at this present,
Now, while I speak this, holds his wife by th'arm,
That little thinks she has been sluiced in's absence,
And his pond fished by his next neighbour, by
Sir Smile, his neighbour. Nay, there's comfort in't
Whiles other men have gates, and those gates opened,

As mine, against their will. Should all despair
That have revolted wives, the tenth of mankind
200 Would hang themselves. Physic for't there's none:
It is a bawdy planet, that will strike
Where 'tis predominant; and 'tis powerful, think it,
From east, west, north, and south. Be it concluded,
No barricado for a belly. Know't:
It will let in and out the enemy
With bag and baggage. Many thousand on's
Have the disease and feel't not. How now, boy?

MAMILLIUS
I am like you, they say.

LEONTES   Why, that's some comfort.
What! Camillo there!

CAMILLO
210 Ay, my good lord.
        He comes forward

LEONTES
Go play, Mamillius. Thou'rt an honest man.
                                Exit Mamillius
Camillo, this great sir will yet stay longer.

CAMILLO
You had much ado to make his anchor hold:
When you cast out, it still came home.

LEONTES   Didst note it?

CAMILLO
He would not stay at your petitions, made
His business more material.

LEONTES   Didst perceive it?
(*aside*) They're here with me already: whispering, round-
        ing,
'Sicilia is a so-forth'. 'Tis far gone
When I shall gust it last. – How came't, Camillo,
That he did stay?

62

CAMILLO At the good Queen's entreaty. 220

LEONTES

'At the Queen's' be't. 'Good' should be pertinent;
But, so it is, it is not. Was this taken
By any understanding pate but thine?
For thy conceit is soaking, will draw in
More than the common blocks. Not noted, is't,
But of the finer natures? By some severals
Of headpiece extraordinary? Lower messes
Perchance are to this business purblind? Say.

CAMILLO

Business, my lord? I think most understand
Bohemia stays here longer.

LEONTES Ha?

CAMILLO Stays here longer. 230

LEONTES

Ay, but why?

CAMILLO

To satisfy your highness, and the entreaties
Of our most gracious mistress.

LEONTES Satisfy?

Th'entreaties of your mistress? Satisfy?
Let that suffice. I have trusted thee, Camillo,
With all the nearest things to my heart, as well
My chamber-counsels, wherein, priestlike, thou
Hast cleansed my bosom, I from thee departed
Thy penitent reformed. But we have been
Deceived in thy integrity, deceived 240
In that which seems so.

CAMILLO Be it forbid, my lord!

LEONTES

To bide upon't: thou art not honest; or
If thou inclin'st that way, thou art a coward,
Which hoxes honesty behind, restraining

From course required. Or else thou must be counted
A servant grafted in my serious trust
And therein negligent, or else a fool
That see'st a game played home, the rich stake drawn,
And tak'st it all for jest.

CAMILLO   My gracious lord,
250 I may be negligent, foolish, and fearful:
In every one of these no man is free,
But that his negligence, his folly, fear,
Among the infinite doings of the world,
Sometime puts forth. In your affairs, my lord,
If ever I were wilful-negligent,
It was my folly; if industriously
I played the fool, it was my negligence,
Not weighing well the end; if ever fearful
To do a thing where I the issue doubted,
260 Whereof the execution did cry out
Against the non-performance, 'twas a fear
Which oft infects the wisest. These, my lord,
Are such allowed infirmities that honesty
Is never free of. But, beseech your grace,
Be plainer with me, let me know my trespass
By its own visage; if I then deny it,
'Tis none of mine.

LEONTES   Ha'not you seen, Camillo –
But that's past doubt, you have, or your eye-glass
Is thicker than a cuckold's horn – or heard –
270 For to a vision so apparent rumour
Cannot be mute – or thought – for cogitation
Resides not in that man that does not think –
My wife is slippery? If thou wilt confess –
Or else be impudently negative
To have nor eyes, nor ears, nor thought – then say
My wife's a hobby-horse, deserves a name

As rank as any flax-wench that puts to
Before her troth-plight: say't and justify't.

CAMILLO

I would not be a stander-by to hear
My sovereign mistress clouded so without   280
My present vengeance taken. 'Shrew my heart,
You never spoke what did become you less
Than this; which to reiterate were sin
As deep as that, though true.

LEONTES   Is whispering nothing?
Is leaning cheek to cheek? Is meeting noses?
Kissing with inside lip? Stopping the career
Of laughter with a sigh? – a note infallible
Of breaking honesty. Horsing foot on foot?
Skulking in corners? Wishing clocks more swift?
Hours minutes? Noon midnight? And all eyes   290
Blind with the pin and web but theirs, theirs only,
That would unseen be wicked – is this nothing?
Why, then the world and all that's in't is nothing;
The covering sky is nothing; Bohemia nothing;
My wife is nothing; nor nothing have these nothings,
If this be nothing.

CAMILLO   Good my lord, be cured
Of this diseased opinion, and betimes,
For 'tis most dangerous.

LEONTES   Say it be, 'tis true.

CAMILLO

No, no, my lord!

LEONTES   It is. You lie, you lie!
I say thou liest, Camillo, and I hate thee,   300
Pronounce thee a gross lout, a mindless slave,
Or else a hovering temporizer, that
Canst with thine eyes at once see good and evil,
Inclining to them both. Were my wife's liver

Infected as her life, she would not live
The running of one glass.

CAMILLO   Who does infect her?

LEONTES

Why, he that wears her like her medal, hanging
About his neck, Bohemia; who, if I
Had servants true about me, that bare eyes
310   To see alike mine honour as their profits,
Their own particular thrifts, they would do that
Which should undo more doing. Ay, and thou,
His cupbearer – whom I from meaner form
Have benched and reared to worship; who mayst see
Plainly as heaven sees earth and earth sees heaven
How I am galled – mightst bespice a cup
To give mine enemy a lasting wink;
Which draught to me were cordial.

CAMILLO   Sir, my lord,
I could do this, and that with no rash potion,
320   But with a lingering dram that should not work
Maliciously, like poison: but I cannot
Believe this crack to be in my dread mistress,
So sovereignly being honourable.
I have loved thee –

LEONTES   Make that thy question, and go rot!
Dost think I am so muddy, so unsettled,
To appoint my self in this vexation; sully
The purity and whiteness of my sheets –
Which to preserve is sleep, which being spotted
Is goads, thorns, nettles, tails of wasps;
330   Give scandal to the blood o'th'Prince, my son –
Who I do think is mine, and love as mine –
Without ripe moving to't? Would I do this?
Could man so blench?

CAMILLO   I must believe you, sir.

I do; and will fetch off Bohemia for't:
Provided that when he's removed your highness
Will take again your queen as yours at first,
Even for your son's sake, and thereby forsealing
The injury of tongues in courts and kingdoms
Known and allied to yours.

LEONTES   Thou dost advise me
Even so as I mine own course have set down.   340
I'll give no blemish to her honour, none.

CAMILLO
My lord,
Go then; and, with a countenance as clear
As friendship wears at feasts, keep with Bohemia
And with your queen. I am his cupbearer.
If from me he have wholesome beverage,
Account me not your servant.

LEONTES   This is all.
Do't and thou hast the one half of my heart;
Do't not, thou split'st thine own.

CAMILLO   I'll do't, my lord.

LEONTES
I will seem friendly, as thou hast advised me.   *Exit* 350

CAMILLO
O miserable lady! But, for me,
What case stand I in? I must be the poisoner
Of good Polixenes, and my ground to do't
Is the obedience to a master – one
Who, in rebellion with himself, will have
All that are his so too. To do this deed,
Promotion follows. If I could find example
Of thousands that had struck anointed kings
And flourished after, I'd not do't; but since
Nor brass, nor stone, nor parchment bears not one,   360
Let villainy itself forswear't. I must

Forsake the court: to do't or no is certain
To me a break-neck. Happy star reign now!
Here comes Bohemia.

Enter Polixenes

POLIXENES   This is strange: methinks
My favour here begins to warp. Not speak?
Good day, Camillo.

CAMILLO   Hail, most royal sir!

POLIXENES
What is the news i'th'court?

CAMILLO   None rare, my lord.

POLIXENES
The King hath on him such a countenance
As he had lost some province, and a region
370 Loved as he loves himself: even now I met him
With customary compliment, when he,
Wafting his eyes to th'contrary, and falling
A lip of much contempt, speeds from me, and
So leaves me to consider what is breeding
That changes thus his manners.

CAMILLO
I dare not know, my lord.

POLIXENES
How, dare not? Do not? Do you know and dare not
Be intelligent to me? 'Tis thereabouts;
For to yourself what you do know you must,
380 And cannot say you dare not. Good Camillo,
Your changed complexions are to me a mirror
Which shows me mine changed too: for I must be
A party in this alteration, finding
Myself thus altered with't.

CAMILLO   There is a sickness
Which puts some of us in distemper, but
I cannot name the disease; and it is caught

68

Of you, that yet are well.

POLIXENES   How! Caught of me?
Make me not sighted like the basilisk.
I have looked on thousands who have sped the better
By my regard, but killed none so. Camillo,   390
As you are certainly a gentleman, thereto
Clerk-like experienced, which no less adorns
Our gentry than our parents' noble names,
In whose success we are gentle: I beseech you,
If you know aught which does behove my knowledge
Thereof to be informed, imprison't not
In ignorant concealment.

CAMILLO   I may not answer.

POLIXENES
A sickness caught of me, and yet I well?
I must be answered. Dost thou hear, Camillo?
I conjure thee, by all the parts of man   400
Which honour does acknowledge, whereof the least
Is not this suit of mine, that thou declare
What incidency thou dost guess of harm
Is creeping toward me; how far off, how near;
Which way to be prevented, if to be;
If not, how best to bear it.

CAMILLO   Sir, I will tell you,
Since I am charged in honour, and by him
That I think honourable. Therefore mark my counsel,
Which must be ev'n as swiftly followed as
I mean to utter it, or both yourself and me   410
Cry lost, and so good night.

POLIXENES   On, good Camillo.

CAMILLO
I am appointed him to murder you.

POLIXENES
By whom, Camillo?

CAMILLO   By the King.
POLIXENES   For what?
CAMILLO
He thinks, nay, with all confidence he swears,
As he had seen't, or been an instrument
To vice you to't, that you have touched his queen
Forbiddenly.
POLIXENES   O, then my best blood turn
To an infected jelly, and my name
Be yoked with his that did betray the Best!
420 Turn then my freshest reputation to
A savour that may strike the dullest nostril
Where I arrive, and my approach be shunned,
Nay, hated too, worse than the great'st infection
That e'er was heard or read!
CAMILLO   Swear his thought over
By each particular star in heaven and
By all their influences, you may as well
Forbid the sea for to obey the moon
As or by oath remove or counsel shake
The fabric of his folly, whose foundation
430 Is piled upon his faith, and will continue
The standing of his body.
POLIXENES   How should this grow?
CAMILLO
I know not; but I am sure 'tis safer to
Avoid what's grown than question how 'tis born.
If therefore you dare trust my honesty,
That lies enclosèd in this trunk, which you
Shall bear along impawned, away tonight!
Your followers I will whisper to the business,
And will by twos and threes, at several posterns,
Clear them o'th'city. For myself, I'll put
440 My fortunes to your service, which are here

By this discovery lost. Be not uncertain,
For, by the honour of my parents, I
Have uttered truth; which if you seek to prove,
I dare not stand by; nor shall you be safer
Than one condemned by the King's own mouth, thereon
His execution sworn.

POLIXENES   I do believe thee:
  I saw his heart in's face. Give me thy hand.
  Be pilot to me, and thy places shall
  Still neighbour mine. My ships are ready, and
  My people did expect my hence departure   450
  Two days ago. This jealousy
  Is for a precious creature; as she's rare
  Must it be great; and as his person's mighty
  Must it be violent; and as he does conceive
  He is dishonoured by a man which ever
  Professed to him, why, his revenges must
  In that be made more bitter. Fear o'ershades me.
  Good expedition be my friend and comfort
  The gracious Queen, part of his theme, but nothing
  Of his ill-ta'en suspicion! Come, Camillo,   460
  I will respect thee as a father if
  Thou bear'st my life off. Hence! Let us avoid.

CAMILLO
  It is in mine authority to command
  The keys of all the posterns. Please your highness
  To take the urgent hour. Come, sir, away.   *Exeunt*

*

Enter Hermione, Mamillius, and Ladies

HERMIONE
> Take the boy to you: he so troubles me,
> 'Tis past enduring.

FIRST LADY   Come, my gracious lord,
> Shall I be your playfellow?

MAMILLIUS   No, I'll none of you.

FIRST LADY
> Why, my sweet lord?

MAMILLIUS
> You'll kiss me hard, and speak to me as if
> I were a baby still. – I love you better.

SECOND LADY
> And why so, my lord?

MAMILLIUS   Not for because
> Your brows are blacker; yet black brows, they say,
> Become some women best, so that there be not
10 Too much hair there, but in a semicircle,
> Or a half-moon, made with a pen.

SECOND LADY   Who taught' this?

MAMILLIUS
> I learned it out of women's faces. Pray now,
> What colour are your eyebrows?

FIRST LADY   Blue, my lord.

MAMILLIUS
> Nay, that's a mock. I have seen a lady's nose
> That has been blue, but not her eyebrows.

FIRST LADY   Hark ye:
> The Queen, your mother, rounds apace. We shall
> Present our services to a fine new prince
> One of these days; and then you'd wanton with us,
> If we would have you.

SECOND LADY   She is spread of late
20 Into a goodly bulk. Good time encounter her!

HERMIONE

    What wisdom stirs amongst you? Come, sir, now
    I am for you again. Pray you, sit by us,
    And tell's a tale.

MAMILLIUS   Merry or sad shall't be?

HERMIONE

    As merry as you will.

MAMILLIUS

    A sad tale's best for winter. I have one
    Of sprites and goblins.

HERMIONE   Let's have that, good sir.
    Come on, sit down; come on, and do your best
    To fright me with your sprites. You're powerful at it.

MAMILLIUS

    There was a man –

HERMIONE   Nay, come sit down; then on.

MAMILLIUS

    Dwelt by a churchyard – I will tell it softly: 30
    Yond crickets shall not hear it.

HERMIONE   Come on, then,
    And give't me in mine ear.

     Enter Leontes, Antigonus, and Lords

LEONTES

    Was he met there? His train? Camillo with him?

LORD

    Behind the tuft of pines I met them. Never
    Saw I men scour so on their way. I eyed them
    Even to their ships.

LEONTES   How blest am I
    In my just censure, in my true opinion!
    Alack, for lesser knowledge! How accursed
    In being so blest! There may be in the cup
    A spider steeped, and one may drink, depart,   40
    And yet partake no venom, for his knowledge

73

Is not infected: but if one present
Th'abhorred ingredient to his eye, make known
How he hath drunk, he cracks his gorge, his sides,
With violent hefts. I have drunk, and seen the spider.
Camillo was his help in this, his pander.
There is a plot against my life, my crown.
All's true that is mistrusted. That false villain
Whom I employed was pre-employed by him.
50   He has discovered my design, and I
Remain a pinched thing; yea, a very trick
For them to play at will. How came the posterns
So easily open?

LORD   By his great authority;
Which often hath no less prevailed than so
On your command.

LEONTES   I know't too well.
(*To Hermione*) Give me the boy. I am glad you did not
        nurse him;
Though he does bear some signs of me, yet you
Have too much blood in him.

HERMIONE   What is this? Sport?

LEONTES

Bear the boy hence; he shall not come about her.
60   Away with him, and let her sport herself
With that she's big with: for 'tis Polixenes
Has made thee swell thus.

        Mamillius is led out

HERMIONE   But I'd say he had not,
And I'll be sworn you would believe my saying,
Howe'er you lean to th'nayward.

LEONTES   You, my lords,
Look on her, mark her well: be but about
To say she is a goodly lady and
The justice of your hearts will thereto add,

74

''Tis pity she's not honest, honourable'.
Praise her but for this her without-door form –
Which, on my faith, deserves high speech – and straight 70
The shrug, the 'hum' or 'ha', these petty brands
That calumny doth use – O, I am out!
That mercy does, for calumny will sear
Virtue itself – these shrugs, these 'hum's and 'ha's,
When you have said she's goodly, come between
Ere you can say she's honest. But be't known,
From him that has most cause to grieve it should be,
She's an adult'ress.

HERMIONE   Should a villain say so,
The most replenished villain in the world,
He were as much more villain. You, my lord,   80
Do but mistake.

LEONTES   You have mistook, my lady,
Polixenes for Leontes. O thou thing
Which I'll not call a creature of thy place,
Lest barbarism, making me the precedent,
Should a like language use to all degrees,
And mannerly distinguishment leave out
Betwixt the prince and beggar. I have said
She's an adult'ress; I have said with whom.
More, she's a traitor, and Camillo is
A fedary with her, and one that knows   90
What she should shame to know herself
But with her most vile principal – that she's
A bed-swerver, even as bad as those
That vulgars give bold'st titles; ay, and privy
To this their late escape.

HERMIONE   No, by my life,
Privy to none of this. How will this grieve you,
When you shall come to clearer knowledge, that
You thus have published me! Gentle my lord,

You scarce can right me throughly then to say
100 You did mistake.

LEONTES   No: if I mistake
In those foundations which I build upon,
The centre is not big enough to bear
A schoolboy's top. Away with her to prison.
He who shall speak for her is afar off guilty
But that he speaks.

HERMIONE   There's some ill planet reigns.
I must be patient till the heavens look
With an aspect more favourable. Good my lords,
I am not prone to weeping, as our sex
Commonly are; the want of which vain dew
110 Perchance shall dry your pities: but I have
That honourable grief lodged here which burns
Worse than tears drown. Beseech you all, my lords,
With thoughts so qualified as your charities
Shall best instruct you measure me; and so
The King's will be performed!

LEONTES   Shall I be heard?

HERMIONE
Who is't that goes with me? Beseech your highness
My women may be with me, for you see
My plight requires it. Do not weep, good fools:
There is no cause. When you shall know your mistress
120 Has deserved prison, then abound in tears
As I come out. This action I now go on
Is for my better grace. Adieu, my lord.
I never wished to see you sorry: now
I trust I shall. My women, come, you have leave.

LEONTES
Go, do our bidding: hence!

                    Exeunt Hermione, guarded, and Ladies

76

LORD
  Beseech your highness, call the Queen again.
ANTIGONUS
  Be certain what you do, sir, lest your justice
  Prove violence, in the which three great ones suffer:
  Yourself, your queen, your son.
LORD   For her, my lord,
  I dare my life lay down, and will do't, sir,   130
  Please you t'accept it, that the Queen is spotless
  I'th'eyes of heaven and to you – I mean
  In this which you accuse her.
ANTIGONUS   If it prove
  She's otherwise, I'll keep my stables where
  I lodge my wife; I'll go in couples with her;
  Than when I feel and see her no farther trust her:
  For every inch of woman in the world,
  Ay, every dram of woman's flesh is false,
  If she be.
LEONTES   Hold your peaces.
LORD   Good my lord –
ANTIGONUS
  It is for you we speak, not for ourselves.   140
  You are abused, and by some putter-on
  That will be damned for't. Would I knew the villain!
  I would lam–damn him. Be she honour-flawed,
  I have three daughters: the eldest is eleven;
  The second and the third nine and some five:
  If this prove true, they'll pay for't. By mine honour,
  I'll geld'em all! Fourteen they shall not see
  To bring false generations. They are co–heirs;
  And I had rather glib myself than they
  Should not produce fair issue.
LEONTES   Cease, no more!   150

77

II.1

You smell this business with a sense as cold
As is a dead man's nose; but I do see't and feel't
As you feel doing thus and see withal
The instruments that feel.

ANTIGONUS   If it be so,
We need no grave to bury honesty:
There's not a grain of it the face to sweeten
Of the whole dungy earth.

LEONTES   What? Lack I credit?

LORD
I had rather you did lack than I, my lord,
Upon this ground; and more it would content me
160 To have her honour true than your suspicion,
Be blamed for't how you might.

LEONTES   Why, what need we
Commune with you of this, but rather follow
Our forceful instigation? Our prerogative
Calls not your counsels, but our natural goodness
Imparts this; which, if you – or stupefied
Or seeming so in skill – cannot or will not
Relish a truth like us, inform yourselves
We need no more of your advice. The matter,
The loss, the gain, the ord'ring on't, is all
170 Properly ours.

ANTIGONUS   And I wish, my liege,
You had only in your silent judgement tried it,
Without more overture.

LEONTES   How could that be?
Either thou art most ignorant by age,
Or thou wert born a fool. Camillo's flight,
Added to their familiarity –
Which was as gross as ever touched conjecture
That lacked sight only, naught for approbation
But only seeing, all other circumstances

78

Made up to th'deed – doth push on this proceeding.
Yet, for a greater confirmation –   180
For in an act of this importance 'twere
Most piteous to be wild – I have dispatched in post
To sacred Delphos, to Apollo's temple,
Cleomenes and Dion, whom you know
Of stuffed sufficiency. Now from the oracle
They will bring all; whose spiritual counsel, had,
Shall stop or spur me. Have I done well?

LORD

Well done, my lord.

LEONTES

Though I am satisfied, and need no more
Than what I know, yet shall the oracle   190
Give rest to th'minds of others, such as he,
Whose ignorant credulity will not
Come up to th'truth. So have we thought it good
From our free person she should be confined,
Lest that the treachery of the two fled hence
Be left her to perform. Come, follow us:
We are to speak in public; for this business
Will raise us all.

ANTIGONUS (*aside*) To laughter, as I take it,
If the good truth were known.

                                                            Exeunt

Enter Paulina, a Gentleman, and Attendants   II.2

PAULINA

The keeper of the prison, call to him.
Let him have knowledge who I am.   *Exit Gentleman*
                                        Good lady,
No court in Europe is too good for thee:
What dost thou then in prison?

79

Enter Gentleman with the Gaoler

                                        Now, good sir,
You know me, do you not?
GAOLER   For a worthy lady,
And one who much I honour.
PAULINA   Pray you, then,
Conduct me to the Queen.
GAOLER   I may not, madam:
To the contrary I have express commandment.
PAULINA
Here's ado
10   To lock up honesty and honour from
Th'access of gentle visitors! Is't lawful, pray you,
To see her women? Any of them? Emilia?
GAOLER
So please you, madam,
To put apart these your attendants, I
Shall bring Emilia forth.
PAULINA   I pray now, call her.
Withdraw yourselves. *Exeunt Gentleman and Attendants*
GAOLER   And, madam,
I must be present at your conference.
PAULINA
Well, be't so, prithee.   *Exit Gaoler*
Here's such ado to make no stain a stain
20   As passes colouring.
        Enter Gaoler with Emilia
                            Dear gentlewoman,
How fares our gracious lady?
EMILIA
As well as one so great and so forlorn
May hold together. On her frights and griefs –
Which never tender lady hath borne greater –
She is something before her time delivered.

PAULINA
  A boy?

EMILIA A daughter, and a goodly babe,
  Lusty, and like to live. The Queen receives
  Much comfort in't; says, 'My poor prisoner,
  I am innocent as you'.

PAULINA   I dare be sworn.
  These dangerous, unsafe lunes i'th'King, beshrew them! 30
  He must be told on't, and he shall. The office
  Becomes a woman best. I'll take't upon me.
  If I prove honey-mouthed, let my tongue blister,
  And never to my red-looked anger be
  The trumpet any more. Pray you, Emilia,
  Commend my best obedience to the Queen.
  If she dares trust me with her little babe,
  I'll show't the King, and undertake to be
  Her advocate to th'loud'st. We do not know
  How he may soften at the sight o'th'child: 40
  The silence often of pure innocence
  Persuades when speaking fails.

EMILIA   Most worthy madam,
  Your honour and your goodness is so evident
  That your free undertaking cannot miss
  A thriving issue. There is no lady living
  So meet for this great errand. Please your ladyship
  To visit the next room, I'll presently
  Acquaint the Queen of your most noble offer,
  Who but today hammered of this design,
  But durst not tempt a minister of honour   50
  Lest she should be denied.

PAULINA   Tell her, Emilia,
  I'll use that tongue I have. If wit flow from't
  As boldness from my bosom, let't not be doubted
  I shall do good.

81

EMILIA　　　　　Now be you blest for it!
I'll to the Queen. Please you come something nearer.

GAOLER
Madam, if't please the Queen to send the babe,
I know not what I shall incur to pass it,
Having no warrant.

PAULINA　　　　You need not fear it, sir.
This child was prisoner to the womb, and is
60　By law and process of great Nature thence
Freed and enfranchised; not a party to
The anger of the King, nor guilty of,
If any be, the trespass of the Queen.

GAOLER
I do believe it.

PAULINA
Do not you fear. Upon mine honour, I
Will stand betwixt you and danger.　　　　*Exeunt*

II.3　　　*Enter Leontes*

LEONTES
Nor night nor day no rest! It is but weakness
To bear the matter thus, mere weakness. If
The cause were not in being – part o'th'cause,
She, th'adult'ress: for the harlot-king
Is quite beyond mine arm, out of the blank
And level of my brain, plot-proof; but she
I can hook to me – say that she were gone,
Given to the fire, a moiety of my rest
Might come to me again. Who's there?
　　　Enter Servant

SERVANT　　　　　　　　　　　My lord?

LEONTES
How does the boy?

SERVANT   He took good rest tonight.   10
'Tis hoped his sickness is discharged.

LEONTES
To see his nobleness!
Conceiving the dishonour of his mother,
He straight declined, drooped, took it deeply,
Fastened and fixed the shame on't in himself;
Threw off his spirit, his appetite, his sleep,
And downright languished. Leave me solely. Go,
See how he fares.   *Exit Servant*
                     Fie, fie, no thought of him!
The very thought of my revenges that way
Recoil upon me: in himself too mighty,   20
And in his parties, his alliance. Let him be
Until a time may serve; for present vengeance
Take it on her. Camillo and Polixenes
Laugh at me, make their pastime at my sorrow.
They should not laugh if I could reach them, nor
Shall she within my power.
          Enter Paulina, carrying a baby, followed by Anti-
          gonus, Lords, and the Servant, who try to prevent her
LORD   You must not enter.

PAULINA
Nay, rather, good my lords, be second to me.
Fear you his tyrannous passion more, alas,
Than the Queen's life? A gracious, innocent soul,
More free than he is jealous.

ANTIGONUS   That's enough.   30

SERVANT
Madam, he hath not slept tonight, commanded
None should come at him.

PAULINA   Not so hot, good sir.
I come to bring him sleep. 'Tis such as you,
That creep like shadows by him, and do sigh

83

At each his needless heavings – such as you
Nourish the cause of his awaking. I
Do come with words as med'cinal as true,
Honest as either, to purge him of that humour
That presses him from sleep.

LEONTES   What noise there, ho?

PAULINA

40 No noise, my lord, but needful conference
About some gossips for your highness.

LEONTES   How?
Away with that audacious lady! Antigonus,
I charged thee that she should not come about me.
I knew she would.

ANTIGONUS   I told her so, my lord,
On your displeasure's peril, and on mine,
She should not visit you.

LEONTES   What? Canst not rule her?

PAULINA

From all dishonesty he can. In this –
Unless he take the course that you have done:
Commit me for committing honour – trust it,
50 He shall not rule me.

ANTIGONUS   La you now, you hear.
When she will take the rein, I let her run;
But she'll not stumble.

PAULINA   Good my liege, I come –
And I beseech you hear me, who professes
Myself your loyal servant, your physician,
Your most obedient counsellor; yet that dares
Less appear so in comforting your evils
Than such as most seem yours – I say, I come
From your good queen.

LEONTES   Good queen?

84

PAULINA

    Good queen, my lord, good queen, I say good queen;

    And would by combat make her good, so were I   60

    A man, the worst about you.

LEONTES   Force her hence.

PAULINA

    Let him that makes but trifles of his eyes

    First hand me. On mine own accord I'll off,

    But first I'll do my errand. The good Queen –

    For she is good – hath brought you forth a daughter:

    Here 'tis; commends it to your blessing.

       She lays down the child

LEONTES   Out!

    A mankind witch! Hence with her, out o'door!

    A most intelligencing bawd!

PAULINA   Not so:

    I am as ignorant in that as you

    In so entitling me; and no less honest   70

    Than you are mad; which is enough, I'll warrant,

    As this world goes, to pass for honest.

LEONTES   Traitors!

    Will you not push her out? Give her the bastard.

    (*To Antigonus*) Thou dotard, thou art woman-tired, un-

          roosted

    By thy Dame Partlet here. Take up the bastard!

    Take't up, I say! Give't to thy crone.

PAULINA   For ever

    Unvenerable be thy hands if thou

    Tak'st up the Princess by that forcèd baseness

    Which he has put upon't!

LEONTES   He dreads his wife.

PAULINA

    So I would you did: then 'twere past all doubt   80

    You'd call your children yours.

LEONTES   A nest of traitors!

ANTIGONUS

    I am none, by this good light!

PAULINA   Nor I, nor any

    But one that's here, and that's himself: for he

    The sacred honour of himself, his queen's,

    His hopeful son's, his babe's, betrays to slander,

    Whose sting is sharper than the sword's; and will not –

    For, as the case now stands, it is a curse

    He cannot be compelled to't – once remove

    The root of his opinion, which is rotten

90   As ever oak or stone was sound.

LEONTES   A callat

    Of boundless tongue, who late hath beat her husband,

    And now baits me! This brat is none of mine:

    It is the issue of Polixenes.

    Hence with it, and together with the dam

    Commit them to the fire!

PAULINA   It is yours;

    And, might we lay th'old proverb to your charge,

    So like you, 'tis the worse. Behold, my lords,

    Although the print be little, the whole matter

    And copy of the father: eye, nose, lip;

100   The trick of's frown; his forehead; nay, the valley,

    The pretty dimples of his chin and cheek; his smiles;

    The very mould and frame of hand, nail, finger.

    And thou, good goddess Nature, which hast made it

    So like to him that got it, if thou hast

    The ordering of the mind too, 'mongst all colours

    No yellow in't, lest she suspect, as he does,

    Her children not her husband's.

LEONTES   A gross hag!

    And, losel, thou art worthy to be hanged,

That wilt not stay her tongue.

ANTIGONUS   Hang all the husbands
That cannot do that feat, you'll leave yourself   110
Hardly one subject.

LEONTES   Once more, take her hence.

PAULINA

A most unworthy and unnatural lord
Can do no more.

LEONTES   I'll ha'thee burned.

PAULINA   I care not:
It is an heretic that makes the fire,
Not she which burns in't. I'll not call you tyrant;
But this most cruel usage of your queen –
Not able to produce more accusation
Than your own weak-hinged fancy – something savours
Of tyranny, and will ignoble make you,
Yea, scandalous to the world.

LEONTES   On your allegiance,   120
Out of the chamber with her! Were I a tyrant,
Where were her life? She durst not call me so,
If she did know me one. Away with her!

          They slowly push her towards the door

PAULINA

I pray you, do not push me, I'll be gone.
Look to your babe, my lord; 'tis yours. Jove send her
A better guiding spirit! What needs these hands?
You that are thus so tender o'er his follies
Will never do him good, not one of you.
So, so. Farewell, we are gone.   *Exit*

LEONTES

Thou, traitor, hast set on thy wife to this.   130
My child? Away with't! Even thou, that hast
A heart so tender o'er it, take it hence
And see it instantly consumed with fire:

Even thou, and none but thou. Take it up straight!
Within this hour bring me word 'tis done,
And by good testimony, or I'll seize thy life,
With what thou else call'st thine. If thou refuse,
And wilt encounter with my wrath, say so:
The bastard brains with these my proper hands
140   Shall I dash out. Go, take it to the fire,
For thou set'st on thy wife.

ANTIGONUS   I did not, sir.
These lords, my noble fellows, if they please,
Can clear me in't.

LORDS   We can. My royal liege,
He is not guilty of her coming hither.

LEONTES
You're liars all.

LORD
Beseech your highness, give us better credit.
We have always truly served you, and beseech'
So to esteem of us; and on our knees we beg,
As recompense of our dear services
150   Past and to come, that you do change this purpose,
Which being so horrible, so bloody, must
Lead on to some foul issue. We all kneel.

LEONTES
I am a feather for each wind that blows.
Shall I live on to see this bastard kneel
And call me father? Better burn it now
Than curse it then. But be it: let it live.
It shall not neither. (*To Antigonus*) You, sir, come you
        hither:
You that have been so tenderly officious
With Lady Margery, your midwife there,
160   To save this bastard's life – for 'tis a bastard,

So sure as this beard's grey – what will you adventure
To save this brat's life?

ANTIGONUS   Anything, my lord,
That my ability may undergo,
And nobleness impose – at least thus much:
I'll pawn the little blood which I have left
To save the innocent – anything possible.

LEONTES
It shall be possible. Swear by this sword
Thou wilt perform my bidding.

ANTIGONUS (*his hand upon the hilt*)
                       I will, my lord.

LEONTES
Mark and perform it, see'st thou? For the fail
Of any point in't shall not only be   170
Death to thyself, but to thy lewd-tongued wife,
Whom for this time we pardon. We enjoin thee,
As thou art liegeman to us, that thou carry
This female bastard hence, and that thou bear it
To some remote and desert place, quite out
Of our dominions; and that there thou leave it,
Without more mercy, to its own protection
And favour of the climate. As by strange fortune
It came to us, I do in justice charge thee,
On thy soul's peril and thy body's torture,   180
That thou commend it strangely to some place
Where chance may nurse or end it. Take it up.

ANTIGONUS
I swear to do this, though a present death
Had been more merciful. Come on, poor babe,
Some powerful spirit instruct the kites and ravens
To be thy nurses! Wolves and bears, they say,
Casting their savageness aside, have done
Like offices of pity. Sir, be prosperous

In more than this deed does require! And blessing
190 Against this cruelty fight on thy side,
Poor thing, condemned to loss!   *Exit with the child*

LEONTES   No, I'll not rear
Another's issue.

    Enter a Servant

SERVANT   Please your highness, posts
From those you sent to th'oracle are come
An hour since: Cleomenes and Dion,
Being well arrived from Delphos, are both landed,
Hasting to th'court.

LORD   So please you, sir, their speed
Hath been beyond accompt.

LEONTES   Twenty-three days
They have been absent. 'Tis good speed; foretells
The great Apollo suddenly will have
200 The truth of this appear. Prepare you, lords.
Summon a session, that we may arraign
Our most disloyal lady: for as she hath
Been publicly accused, so shall she have
A just and open trial. While she lives
My heart will be a burden to me. Leave me,
And think upon my bidding.   *Exeunt*

III.1   *Enter Cleomenes and Dion*

CLEOMENES
The climate's delicate, the air most sweet,
Fertile the isle, the temple much surpassing
The common praise it bears.

DION   I shall report,
For most it caught me, the celestial habits –

Methinks I so should term them – and the reverence
Of the grave wearers. O, the sacrifice!
How ceremonious, solemn, and unearthly
It was i'th'off'ring!

CLEOMENES   But of all, the burst
And the ear-deaf'ning voice o'th'oracle,
Kin to Jove's thunder, so surprised my sense   10
That I was nothing.

DION   If th'event o'th'journey
Prove as successful to the Queen – O, be't so! –
As it hath been to us rare, pleasant, speedy,
The time is worth the use on't.

CLEOMENES   Great Apollo
Turn all to th'best! These proclamations,
So forcing faults upon Hermione,
I little like.

DION   The violent carriage of it
Will clear or end the business. When the oracle,
Thus by Apollo's great divine sealed up,
Shall the contents discover, something rare   20
Even then will rush to knowledge. Go: fresh horses!
And gracious be the issue.   *Exeunt*

                Enter Leontes, Lords, and Officers   III.2

LEONTES
This sessions, to our great grief we pronounce,
Even pushes 'gainst our heart: the party tried
The daughter of a king, our wife, and one
Of us too much beloved. Let us be cleared
Of being tyrannous, since we so openly
Proceed in justice, which shall have due course,
Even to the guilt or the purgation.
Produce the prisoner.

91

III.2

OFFICER

It is his highness' pleasure that the Queen
10   Appear in person here in court.

Enter Hermione, guarded, Paulina, and Ladies attending

Silence!

LEONTES

Read the indictment.

OFFICER (*reads*) *Hermione, Queen to the worthy Leontes,
King of Sicilia, thou art here accused and arraigned of high
treason, in committing adultery with Polixenes, King of
Bohemia, and conspiring with Camillo to take away the
life of our sovereign lord the King, thy royal husband;
the pretence whereof being by circumstances partly laid
open, thou, Hermione, contrary to the faith and allegiance
of a true subject, didst counsel and aid them, for their*
20   *better safety, to fly away by night.*

HERMIONE

Since what I am to say must be but that
Which contradicts my accusation, and
The testimony on my part no other
But what comes from myself, it shall scarce boot me
To say 'Not guilty': mine integrity
Being counted falsehood, shall, as I express it,
Be so received. But thus: if powers divine
Behold our human actions – as they do –
I doubt not then but innocence shall make
30   False accusation blush, and tyranny
Tremble at patience. You, my lord, best know –
Who least will seem to do so – my past life
Hath been as continent, as chaste, as true,
As I am now unhappy; which is more
Than history can pattern, though devised
And played to take spectators. For behold me,

A fellow of the royal bed, which owe
A moiety of the throne, a great king's daughter,
The mother to a hopeful prince, here standing
To prate and talk for life and honour 'fore   40
Who please to come and hear. For life, I prize it
As I weigh grief, which I would spare; for honour,
'Tis a derivative from me to mine,
And only that I stand for. I appeal
To your own conscience, sir, before Polixenes
Came to your court, how I was in your grace,
How merited to be so; since he came,
With what encounter so uncurrent I
Have strained t'appear thus: if one jot beyond
The bound of honour, or in act or will   50
That way inclining, hardened be the hearts
Of all that hear me, and my near'st of kin
Cry fie upon my grave!

LEONTES   I ne'er heard yet
That any of these bolder vices wanted
Less impudence to gainsay what they did
Than to perform it first.

HERMIONE   That's true enough,
Though 'tis a saying, sir, not due to me.

LEONTES
You will not own it.

HERMIONE   More than mistress of
Which comes to me in name of fault I must not
At all acknowledge. For Polixenes,   60
With whom I am accused, I do confess
I loved him as in honour he required:
With such a kind of love as might become
A lady like me; with a love even such,
So and no other, as yourself commanded;
Which not to have done I think had been in me

93

Both disobedience and ingratitude
To you and toward your friend, whose love had spoke
Even since it could speak, from an infant, freely
70 That it was yours. Now, for conspiracy,
I know not how it tastes, though it be dished
For me to try how. All I know of it
Is that Camillo was an honest man;
And why he left your court the gods themselves,
Wotting no more than I, are ignorant.

LEONTES
You knew of his departure, as you know
What you have underta'en to do in's absence.

HERMIONE
Sir,
You speak a language that I understand not.
80 My life stands in the level of your dreams,
Which I'll lay down.

LEONTES   Your actions are my dreams.
You had a bastard by Polixenes,
And I but dreamed it. As you were past all shame –
Those of your fact are so – so past all truth;
Which to deny concerns more than avails: for as
Thy brat hath been cast out, like to itself,
No father owning it – which is indeed
More criminal in thee than it – so thou
Shalt feel our justice, in whose easiest passage
90 Look for no less than death.

HERMIONE   Sir, spare your threats!
The bug which you would fright me with I seek.
To me can life be no commodity:
The crown and comfort of my life, your favour,
I do give lost, for I do feel it gone,
But know not how it went. My second joy,
And first-fruits of my body, from his presence

I am barred, like one infectious. My third comfort,
Starred most unluckily, is from my breast –
The innocent milk in its most innocent mouth –
Haled out to murder. Myself on every post   100
Proclaimed a strumpet; with immodest hatred
The childbed privilege denied, which 'longs
To women of all fashion; lastly, hurried
Here to this place, i'th'open air, before
I have got strength of limit. Now, my liege,
Tell me what blessings I have here alive
That I should fear to die. Therefore proceed.
But yet hear this – mistake me not: no life,
I prize it not a straw; but for mine honour,
Which I would free – if I shall be condemned   110
Upon surmises, all proofs sleeping else
But what your jealousies awake, I tell you
'Tis rigour and not law. Your honours all,
I do refer me to the oracle:
Apollo be my judge!

LORD   This your request
Is altogether just. Therefore bring forth,
And in Apollo's name, his oracle. *Exeunt certain Officers*

HERMIONE

The Emperor of Russia was my father.
O that he were alive, and here beholding
His daughter's trial! That he did but see   120
The flatness of my misery; yet with eyes
Of pity, not revenge!

    Enter Officers, with Cleomenes and Dion

OFFICER

You here shall swear upon this sword of justice
That you, Cleomenes and Dion, have
Been both at Delphos, and from thence have brought
This sealed-up oracle, by the hand delivered

Of great Apollo's priest; and that since then
You have not dared to break the holy seal,
Nor read the secrets in't.

CLEOMENES *and* DION   All this we swear.

LEONTES

130 Break up the seals and read.

OFFICER (*reads*) *Hermione is chaste; Polixenes blameless;
Camillo a true subject; Leontes a jealous tyrant; his innocent babe truly begotten; and the King shall live without
an heir, if that which is lost be not found.*

LORDS

Now blessèd be the great Apollo!

HERMIONE   Praised!

LEONTES

Hast thou read truth?

OFFICER   Ay, my lord, even so
As it is here set down.

LEONTES

There is no truth at all i'th'oracle!
The sessions shall proceed: this is mere falsehood.
    Enter Servant

SERVANT

140 My lord the King, the King!

LEONTES   What is the business?

SERVANT

O sir, I shall be hated to report it:
The Prince your son, with mere conceit and fear
Of the Queen's speed, is gone.

LEONTES   How! Gone?

SERVANT   Is dead.

LEONTES

Apollo's angry, and the heavens themselves
Do strike at my injustice.
    Hermione faints

How now there!

PAULINA

This news is mortal to the Queen: look down
And see what death is doing.

LEONTES   Take her hence.
Her heart is but o'ercharged; she will recover.
I have too much believed mine own suspicion.
Beseech you, tenderly apply to her   150
Some remedies for life.

Exeunt Paulina and Ladies, bearing Hermione
Apollo, pardon
My great profaneness 'gainst thine oracle!
I'll reconcile me to Polixenes;
New woo my queen; recall the good Camillo –
Whom I proclaim a man of truth, of mercy:
For, being transported by my jealousies
To bloody thoughts and to revenge, I chose
Camillo for the minister to poison
My friend Polixenes; which had been done,
But that the good mind of Camillo tardied   160
My swift command, though I with death and with
Reward did threaten and encourage him,
Not doing it and being done. He, most humane,
And filled with honour, to my kingly guest
Unclasped my practice, quit his fortunes here –
Which you knew great – and to the hazard
Of all incertainties himself commended,
No richer than his honour. How he glisters
Through my rust! And how his piety
Does my deeds make the blacker!

Enter Paulina

PAULINA   Woe the while!   170
O cut my lace, lest my heart, cracking it,
Break too!

97

LORD   What fit is this, good lady?

PAULINA

What studied torments, tyrant, hast for me?
What wheels? Racks? Fires? What flaying? Boiling
In leads or oils? What old or newer torture
Must I receive, whose every word deserves
To taste of thy most worst? Thy tyranny,
Together working with thy jealousies –
Fancies too weak for boys, too green and idle

180   For girls of nine – O think what they have done,
And then run mad indeed, stark mad! For all
Thy bygone fooleries were but spices of it.
That thou betrayedst Polixenes 'twas nothing:
That did but show thee of a fool inconstant,
And damnable ingrateful. Nor was't much
Thou wouldst have poisoned good Camillo's honour
To have him kill a king – poor trespasses,
More monstrous standing by: whereof I reckon
The casting forth to crows thy baby daughter

190   To be or none or little, though a devil
Would have shed water out of fire ere done't;
Nor is't directly laid to thee, the death
Of the young Prince, whose honourable thoughts –
Thoughts high for one so tender – cleft the heart
That could conceive a gross and foolish sire
Blemished his gracious dam. This is not, no,
Laid to thy answer. But the last – O lords,
When I have said, cry woe! The Queen, the Queen,
The sweet'st, dear'st creature's dead! And vengeance
         for't

200   Not dropped down yet.

LORDS   The higher powers forbid!

PAULINA

I say she's dead; I'll swear't. If word nor oath

98

Prevail not, go and see. If you can bring
Tincture or lustre in her lip, her eye,
Heat outwardly or breath within, I'll serve you
As I would do the gods. But, O thou tyrant,
Do not repent these things, for they are heavier
Than all thy woes can stir. Therefore betake thee
To nothing but despair. A thousand knees,
Ten thousand years together, naked, fasting,
Upon a barren mountain, and still winter   210
In storm perpetual, could not move the gods
To look that way thou wert.

LEONTES   Go on, go on:
Thou canst not speak too much; I have deserved
All tongues to talk their bitt'rest.

LORD   Say no more.
Howe'er the business goes, you have made fault
I'th'boldness of your speech.

PAULINA   I am sorry for't.
All faults I make, when I shall come to know them,
I do repent. Alas, I have showed too much
The rashness of a woman! He is touched
To th'noble heart. What's gone and what's past help   220
Should be past grief. Do not receive affliction
At my petition, I beseech you; rather
Let me be punished, that have minded you
Of what you should forget. Now, good my liege,
Sir, royal sir, forgive a foolish woman.
The love I bore your queen – lo, fool again!
I'll speak of her no more, nor of your children;
I'll not remember you of my own lord,
Who is lost too. Take your patience to you,
And I'll say nothing.

LEONTES   Thou didst speak but well   230
When most the truth; which I receive much better

99

Than to be pitied of thee. Prithee, bring me
To the dead bodies of my queen and son.
One grave shall be for both: upon them shall
The causes of their death appear, unto
Our shame perpetual. Once a day I'll visit
The chapel where they lie, and tears shed there
Shall be my recreation. So long as nature
Will bear up with this exercise, so long
240 I daily vow to use it. Come,
And lead me to these sorrows.   *Exeunt*

III.3   *Enter Antigonus with the child, and a Mariner*

ANTIGONUS
Thou art perfect, then, our ship hath touched upon
The deserts of Bohemia?

MARINER   Ay, my lord, and fear
We have landed in ill time: the skies look grimly,
And threaten present blusters. In my conscience,
The heavens with that we have in hand are angry
And frown upon's.

ANTIGONUS
Their sacred wills be done! Go, get aboard;
Look to thy bark. I'll not be long before
I call upon thee.

MARINER   Make your best haste, and go not
10 Too far i'th'land: 'tis like to be loud weather.
Besides, this place is famous for the creatures
Of prey that keep upon't.

ANTIGONUS   Go thou away:
I'll follow instantly.

MARINER   I am glad at heart
To be so rid o'th'business.   *Exit*

ANTIGONUS   Come, poor babe.

I have heard, but not believed, the spirits o'th'dead
May walk again: if such thing be, thy mother
Appeared to me last night; for ne'er was dream
So like a waking. To me comes a creature,
Sometimes her head on one side, some another:
I never saw a vessel of like sorrow,   20
So filled and so becoming. In pure white robes,
Like very sanctity, she did approach
My cabin where I lay; thrice bowed before me,
And, gasping to begin some speech, her eyes
Became two spouts; the fury spent, anon
Did this break from her: 'Good Antigonus,
Since fate, against thy better disposition,
Hath made thy person for the thrower-out
Of my poor babe, according to thy oath,
Places remote enough are in Bohemia: 30
There weep, and leave it crying; and for the babe
Is counted lost for ever, Perdita
I prithee call't. For this ungentle business,
Put on thee by my lord, thou ne'er shalt see
Thy wife Paulina more.' And so, with shrieks,
She melted into air. Affrighted much,
I did in time collect myself, and thought
This was so, and no slumber. Dreams are toys:
Yet for this once, yea superstitiously,
I will be squared by this. I do believe   40
Hermione hath suffered death, and that
Apollo would, this being indeed the issue
Of King Polixenes, it should here be laid,
Either for life or death, upon the earth
Of its right father. Blossom, speed thee well!
           He lays down the child, and a scroll
There lie, and there thy character;
           (he lays down a box)

there these,
Which may, if fortune please, both breed thee, pretty,
And still rest thine. The storm begins. Poor wretch,
That for thy mother's fault art thus exposed
50 To loss and what may follow! Weep I cannot,
But my heart bleeds; and most accursed am I
To be by oath enjoined to this. Farewell!
The day frowns more and more. Thou'rt like to have
A lullaby too rough: I never saw
The heavens so dim by day. – A savage clamour!
Well may I get aboard! This is the chase.
I am gone for ever!   *Exit, pursued by a bear*
      Enter an old Shepherd

SHEPHERD I would there were no age between ten and
  three-and-twenty, or that youth would sleep out the
60 rest: for there is nothing in the between but getting
  wenches with child, wronging the ancientry, stealing,
  fighting. Hark you now: would any but these boiled
  brains of nineteen and two-and-twenty hunt this
  weather? They have scared away two of my best sheep,
  which I fear the wolf will sooner find than the master. If
  anywhere I have them, 'tis by the seaside, browsing of
  ivy. Good luck, an't be thy will!
      He sees the child
  What have we here? Mercy on's, a barne! A very pretty
  barne. A boy or a child, I wonder? A pretty one, a very
70 pretty one. Sure, some scape. Though I am not bookish,
  yet I can read waiting gentlewoman in the scape: this
  has been some stair-work, some trunk-work, some behind-door-work. They were warmer that got this than
  the poor thing is here. I'll take it up for pity – yet I'll
  tarry till my son come: he hallowed but even now. Whoa-
  ho-hoa!
      Enter Clown

CLOWN Hilloa, loa!

SHEPHERD What! Art so near? If thou'lt see a thing to
talk on when thou art dead and rotten, come hither.
What ail'st thou, man?   80

CLOWN I have seen two such sights, by sea and by land!
But I am not to say it is a sea, for it is now the sky: betwixt the firmament and it you cannot thrust a bodkin's
point.

SHEPHERD Why, boy, how is it?

CLOWN I would you did but see how it chafes, how it
rages, how it takes up the shore – but that's not to the
point. O, the most piteous cry of the poor souls! Sometimes to see 'em, and not to see 'em: now the ship boring
the moon with her mainmast, and anon swallowed with   90
yeast and froth, as you'd thrust a cork into a hogshead.
And then for the land-service: to see how the bear tore
out his shoulder bone, how he cried to me for help, and
said his name was Antigonus, a nobleman. But to make
an end of the ship: to see how the sea flap-dragoned it;
but first, how the poor souls roared, and the sea mocked
them; and how the poor gentleman roared, and the bear
mocked him, both roaring louder than the sea or weather.

SHEPHERD Name of mercy, when was this, boy?

CLOWN Now, now! I have not winked since I saw these   100
sights. The men are not yet cold under water, nor the
bear half dined on the gentleman; he's at it now.

SHEPHERD Would I had been by, to have helped the old
man!

CLOWN I would you had been by the ship side, to have
helped her: there your charity would have lacked
footing.

SHEPHERD Heavy matters, heavy matters! But look thee
here, boy. Now bless thyself: thou met'st with things
dying, I with things new-born. Here's a sight for thee: 110

look thee, a bearing-cloth for a squire's child! Look thee here!

He points to the box

Take up, take up, boy; open it. So, let's see. It was told me I should be rich by the fairies. This is some change-ling. Open't. What's within, boy?

CLOWN (*opening the box*) You're a made old man. If the sins of your youth are forgiven you, you're well to live. Gold! All gold!

SHEPHERD This is fairy gold, boy, and 'twill prove so. Up
120 with't, keep it close. Home, home, the next way! We are lucky, boy, and to be so still requires nothing but secrecy. Let my sheep go! Come, good boy, the next way home.

CLOWN Go you the next way with your findings. I'll go see if the bear be gone from the gentleman, and how much he hath eaten. They are never curst but when they are hungry. If there be any of him left, I'll bury it.

SHEPHERD That's a good deed. If thou mayst discern by that which is left of him what he is, fetch me to th'sight
130 of him.

CLOWN Marry will I; and you shall help to put him i'th'ground.

SHEPHERD 'Tis a lucky day, boy, and we'll do good deeds on't. *Exeunt*

❋

IV.1 *Enter Time, the Chorus*

TIME

I that please some, try all; both joy and terror
Of good and bad; that makes and unfolds error,

Now take upon me, in the name of Time,
To use my wings. Impute it not a crime
To me or my swift passage that I slide
O'er sixteen years, and leave the growth untried
Of that wide gap, since it is in my power
To o'erthrow law, and in one self-born hour
To plant and o'erwhelm custom. Let me pass
The same I am ere ancient'st order was   10
Or what is now received. I witness to
The times that brought them in; so shall I do
To th'freshest things now reigning, and make stale
The glistering of this present, as my tale
Now seems to it. Your patience this allowing,
I turn my glass, and give my scene such growing
As you had slept between. Leontes leaving –
Th'effects of his fond jealousies so grieving
That he shuts up himself – imagine me,
Gentle spectators, that I now may be   20
In fair Bohemia; and remember well,
I mentioned a son o'th'King's, which Florizel
I now name to you; and with speed so pace
To speak of Perdita, now grown in grace
Equal with wond'ring. What of her ensues
I list not prophesy; but let Time's news
Be known when 'tis brought forth. A shepherd's
            daughter,
And what to her adheres, which follows after,
Is th'argument of Time. Of this allow,
If ever you have spent time worse ere now;   30
If never, yet that Time himself doth say
He wishes earnestly you never may.   *Exit*

105

POLIXENES I pray thee, good Camillo, be no more im-
portunate. 'Tis a sickness denying thee anything; a
death to grant this.

CAMILLO It is fifteen years since I saw my country.
Though I have for the most part been aired abroad, I
desire to lay my bones there. Besides, the penitent King,
my master, hath sent for me; to whose feeling sorrows I
might be some allay – or I o'erween to think so – which
is another spur to my departure.

10 POLIXENES As thou lov'st me, Camillo, wipe not out the
rest of thy services by leaving me now. The need I have
of thee thine own goodness hath made. Better not to
have had thee than thus to want thee. Thou, having
made me businesses which none without thee can
sufficiently manage, must either stay to execute them
thyself or take away with thee the very services thou hast
done; which, if I have not enough considered – as too
much I cannot – to be more thankful to thee shall be my
study, and my profit therein the heaping friendships. Of
20 that fatal country, Sicilia, prithee speak no more, whose
very naming punishes me with the remembrance of that
penitent, as thou call'st him, and reconciled king, my
brother; whose loss of his most precious queen and
children are even now to be afresh lamented. Say to me,
when saw'st thou the Prince Florizel, my son? Kings
are no less unhappy, their issue not being gracious, than
they are in losing them when they have approved their
virtues.

CAMILLO Sir, it is three days since I saw the Prince. What
30 his happier affairs may be are to me unknown; but I
have missingly noted he is of late much retired from
court, and is less frequent to his princely exercises than
formerly he hath appeared.

POLIXENES I have considered so much, Camillo, and
with some care; so far that I have eyes under my service
which look upon his removedness, from whom I have
this intelligence: that he is seldom from the house of a
most homely shepherd – a man, they say, that from very
nothing, and beyond the imagination of his neighbours,
is grown into an unspeakable estate. 40

CAMILLO I have heard, sir, of such a man, who hath a
daughter of most rare note: the report of her is extended
more than can be thought to begin from such a cottage.

POLIXENES That's likewise part of my intelligence, but, I
fear, the angle that plucks our son thither. Thou shalt
accompany us to the place, where we will, not appearing
what we are, have some question with the shepherd;
from whose simplicity I think it not uneasy to get the
cause of my son's resort thither. Prithee be my present
partner in this business, and lay aside the thoughts of 50
Sicilia.

CAMILLO I willingly obey your command.

POLIXENES My best Camillo! We must disguise ourselves. *Exeunt*

Enter Autolycus, singing IV.3
AUTOLYCUS
When daffodils begin to peer,
With heigh, the doxy over the dale,
Why, then comes in the sweet o'the year,
For the red blood reigns in the winter's pale.

The white sheet bleaching on the hedge,
With heigh, the sweet birds O, how they sing!
Doth set my pugging tooth an edge,
For a quart of ale is a dish for a king.

10   The lark, that tirra-lyra chants,
          With heigh, with heigh, the thrush and the jay,
      Are summer songs for me and my aunts
          While we lie tumbling in the hay.

      I have served Prince Florizel, and in my time wore
      three-pile; but now I am out of service.

      But shall I go mourn for that, my dear?
          The pale moon shines by night:
      And when I wander here and there
          I then do most go right.

20   If tinkers may have leave to live,
          And bear the sow-skin budget,
      Then my account I well may give,
          And in the stocks avouch it.

      My traffic is sheets; when the kite builds, look to lesser
      linen. My father named me Autolycus, who, being, as I
      am, littered under Mercury, was likewise a snapper-up
      of unconsidered trifles. With die and drab I purchased
      this caparison, and my revenue is the silly cheat. Gal-
      lows and knock are too powerful on the highway: beat-
      ing and hanging are terrors to me. For the life to come, I
30   sleep out the thought of it. A prize! A prize!
          Enter Clown
      CLOWN Let me see: every 'leven wether tods, every tod
      yields pound and odd shilling; fifteen hundred shorn,
      what comes the wool to?
      AUTOLYCUS (*aside*) If the springe hold, the cock's mine.
      CLOWN I cannot do't without counters. Let me see: what
      am I to buy for our sheep-shearing feast? Three pound
      of sugar, five pound of currants, rice – what will this

sister of mine do with rice? But my father hath made her mistress of the feast, and she lays it on. She hath made me four-and-twenty nosegays for the shearers, three-man-song men all, and very good ones; but they are most of them means and basses – but one Puritan amongst them, and he sings psalms to hornpipes. I must have saffron to colour the warden pies; mace; dates – none, that's out of my note; nutmegs, seven; a race or two of ginger, but that I may beg; four pound of prunes, and as many of raisins o'th'sun.

AUTOLYCUS (*grovelling on the ground*) O that ever I was born!

CLOWN I'th'name of me!

AUTOLYCUS O, help me, help me! Pluck but off these rags; and then death, death!

CLOWN Alack, poor soul! Thou hast need of more rags to lay on thee, rather than have these off.

AUTOLYCUS O sir, the loathsomeness of them offend me more than the stripes I have received, which are mighty ones and millions.

CLOWN Alas, poor man! A million of beating may come to a great matter.

AUTOLYCUS I am robbed, sir, and beaten; my money and apparel ta'en from me, and these detestable things put upon me.

CLOWN What, by a horseman or a footman?

AUTOLYCUS A footman, sweet sir, a footman.

CLOWN Indeed, he should be a footman, by the garments he has left with thee. If this be a horseman's coat, it hath seen very hot service. Lend me thy hand, I'll help thee. Come, lend me thy hand.

    He helps him up

AUTOLYCUS O, good sir, tenderly, O!

CLOWN Alas, poor soul!

AUTOLYCUS O, good sir, softly, good sir! I fear, sir, my shoulder-blade is out.

CLOWN How now? Canst stand?

AUTOLYCUS Softly, dear sir; (*he picks his pockets*) good sir, softly. You ha'done me a charitable office.

CLOWN Dost lack any money? I have a little money for thee.

AUTOLYCUS No, good, sweet sir; no, I beseech you, sir. I have a kinsman not past three-quarters of a mile hence, 80 unto whom I was going. I shall there have money, or anything I want. Offer me no money, I pray you: that kills my heart.

CLOWN What manner of fellow was he that robbed you?

AUTOLYCUS A fellow, sir, that I have known to go about with troll-my-dames. I knew him once a servant of the Prince. I cannot tell, good sir, for which of his virtues it was, but he was certainly whipped out of the court.

CLOWN His vices, you would say. There's no virtue whipped out of the court: they cherish it to make it stay 90 there; and yet it will no more but abide.

AUTOLYCUS Vices I would say, sir. I know this man well. He hath been since an ape-bearer; then a process-server, a bailiff; then he compassed a motion of the Prodigal Son, and married a tinker's wife within a mile where my land and living lies; and having flown over many knavish professions, he settled only in rogue. Some call him Autolycus.

CLOWN Out upon him! Prig, for my life, prig! He haunts wakes, fairs, and bear-baitings.

100 AUTOLYCUS Very true, sir; he, sir, he: that's the rogue that put me into this apparel.

CLOWN Not a more cowardly rogue in all Bohemia. If you had but looked big and spit at him, he'd have run.

AUTOLYCUS I must confess to you, sir, I am no fighter.

I am false of heart that way, and that he knew, I warrant
him.

CLOWN How do you now?

AUTOLYCUS Sweet sir, much better than I was: I can
stand and walk. I will even take my leave of you, and
pace softly towards my kinsman's.   110

CLOWN Shall I bring thee on the way?

AUTOLYCUS No, good-faced sir; no, sweet sir.

CLOWN Then fare thee well. I must go buy spices for our
sheep-shearing.

AUTOLYCUS Prosper you, sweet sir!   *Exit Clown*
Your purse is not hot enough to purchase your spice.
I'll be with you at your sheep-shearing too. If I make
not this cheat bring out another, and the shearers prove
sheep, let me be unrolled, and my name put in the book
of virtue! (*sings*)   120

> Jog on, jog on, the footpath way,
>   And merrily hent the stile-a:
> A merry heart goes all the day,
>   Your sad tires in a mile-a.   *Exit*

Enter Florizel and Perdita   IV.4

FLORIZEL
These your unusual weeds to each part of you
Does give a life: no shepherdess, but Flora
Peering in April's front. This your sheep-shearing
Is as a meeting of the petty gods,
And you the queen on't.

PERDITA   Sir, my gracious lord,
To chide at your extremes it not becomes me –
O, pardon that I name them: your high self,
The gracious mark o'th'land, you have obscured
With a swain's wearing, and me, poor lowly maid,

10 Most goddess-like pranked up. But that our feasts
In every mess have folly, and the feeders
Digest it with accustom, I should blush
To see you so attired, swoon, I think,
To show myself a glass.

FLORIZEL   I bless the time
When my good falcon made her flight across
Thy father's ground.

PERDITA   Now Jove afford you cause!
To me the difference forges dread; your greatness
Hath not been used to fear. Even now I tremble
To think your father by some accident
20 Should pass this way, as you did. O, the Fates!
How would he look to see his work, so noble,
Vilely bound up? What would he say? Or how
Should I, in these my borrowed flaunts, behold
The sternness of his presence?

FLORIZEL   Apprehend
Nothing but jollity. The gods themselves,
Humbling their deities to love, have taken
The shapes of beasts upon them: Jupiter
Became a bull, and bellowed; the green Neptune
A ram, and bleated; and the fire-robed god,
30 Golden Apollo, a poor, humble swain,
As I seem now. Their transformations
Were never for a piece of beauty rarer,
Nor in a way so chaste, since my desires
Run not before mine honour, nor my lusts
Burn hotter than my faith.

PERDITA   O, but sir,
Your resolution cannot hold when 'tis
Opposed, as it must be, by th'power of the King.
One of these two must be necessities,

Which then will speak: that you must change this pur-
    pose
Or I my life.

FLORIZEL   Thou dearest Perdita,   40
With these forced thoughts, I prithee, darken not
The mirth o'th'feast. Or I'll be thine, my fair,
Or not my father's. For I cannot be
Mine own, nor anything to any, if
I be not thine. To this I am most constant,
Though destiny say no. Be merry, gentle;
Strangle such thoughts as these with anything
That you behold the while. Your guests are coming:
Lift up your countenance as it were the day
Of celebration of that nuptial which   50
We two have sworn shall come.

PERDITA   O lady Fortune,
Stand you auspicious!

FLORIZEL   See, your guests approach.
Address yourself to entertain them sprightly,
And let's be red with mirth.

    Enter Shepherd, with Polixenes and Camillo, dis-
    guised; Clown, Mopsa, Dorcas, and others

SHEPHERD
Fie, daughter! When my old wife lived, upon
This day she was both pantler, butler, cook;
Both dame and servant; welcomed all, served all;
Would sing her song and dance her turn; now here,
At upper end o'th'table, now i'th'middle;
On his shoulder, and his; her face o'fire   60
With labour, and the thing she took to quench it:
She would to each one sip. You are retired,
As if you were a feasted one and not
The hostess of the meeting. Pray you, bid

These unknown friends to's welcome, for it is
A way to make us better friends, more known.
Come, quench your blushes and present yourself
That which you are, Mistress o'th'Feast. Come on,
And bid us welcome to your sheep-shearing,
70 As your good flock shall prosper.

PERDITA (*to Polixenes*)   Sir, welcome.
It is my father's will I should take on me
The hostess-ship o'th'day. (*To Camillo*) You're welcome,
        sir.
Give me those flowers there, Dorcas. Reverend sirs,
For you there's rosemary and rue; these keep
Seeming and savour all the winter long:
Grace and remembrance be to you both,
And welcome to our shearing!

POLIXENES   Shepherdess –
A fair one are you – well you fit our ages
With flowers of winter.

PERDITA   Sir, the year growing ancient,
80 Not yet on summer's death nor on the birth
Of trembling winter, the fairest flowers o'th'season
Are our carnations and streaked gillyvors,
Which some call Nature's bastards; of that kind
Our rustic garden's barren, and I care not
To get slips of them.

POLIXENES   Wherefore, gentle maiden,
Do you neglect them?

PERDITA   For I have heard it said
There is an art which in their piedness shares
With great creating Nature.

POLIXENES   Say there be;
Yet Nature is made better by no mean
90 But Nature makes that mean; so over that art
Which you say adds to Nature is an art

114

That Nature makes. You see, sweet maid, we marry
A gentler scion to the wildest stock,
And make conceive a bark of baser kind
By bud of nobler race. This is an art
Which does mend Nature – change it, rather – but
The art itself is Nature.

PERDITA   So it is.

POLIXENES

Then make your garden rich in gillyvors,
And do not call them bastards.

PERDITA   I'll not put
The dibble in earth to set one slip of them: 100
No more than, were I painted, I would wish
This youth should say 'twere well, and only therefore
Desire to breed by me. Here's flowers for you:
Hot lavender, mints, savory, marjoram;
The marigold, that goes to bed with' sun
And with him rises weeping; these are flowers
Of middle summer, and I think they are given
To men of middle age. Y'are very welcome.

CAMILLO

I should leave grazing, were I of your flock,
And only live by gazing.

PERDITA   Out, alas!   110
You'd be so lean that blasts of January
Would blow you through and through. (*To Florizel*)
          Now, my fair'st friend,
I would I had some flowers o'th'spring, that might
Become your time of day – (*to the Shepherdesses*) and
          yours, and yours,
That wear upon your virgin branches yet
Your maidenheads growing. O Proserpina,
For the flowers now that, frighted, thou let'st fall
From Dis's wagon! Daffodils,

That come before the swallow dares, and take
120 The winds of March with beauty; violets, dim,
But sweeter than the lids of Juno's eyes
Or Cytherea's breath; pale primroses,
That die unmarried ere they can behold
Bright Phoebus in his strength – a malady
Most incident to maids; bold oxlips and
The crown imperial; lilies of all kinds,
The flower-de-luce being one: O, these I lack
To make you garlands of, and my sweet friend
To strew him o'er and o'er!

FLORIZEL   What, like a corse?

PERDITA
130 No, like a bank for Love to lie and play on,
Not like a corse; or if, not to be buried,
But quick and in mine arms. Come, take your flowers.
Methinks I play as I have seen them do
In Whitsun pastorals: sure this robe of mine
Does change my disposition.

FLORIZEL   What you do
Still betters what is done. When you speak, sweet,
I'd have you do it ever; when you sing,
I'd have you buy and sell so, so give alms,
Pray so, and, for the ord'ring your affairs,
140 To sing them too; when you do dance, I wish you
A wave o'th'sea, that you might ever do
Nothing but that – move still, still so,
And own no other function. Each your doing,
So singular in each particular,
Crowns what you are doing in the present deeds,
That all your acts are queens.

PERDITA   O Doricles,
Your praises are too large. But that your youth
And the true blood which peeps fairly through't

Do plainly give you out an unstained shepherd,
With wisdom I might fear, my Doricles,   150
You wooed me the false way.

FLORIZEL   I think you have
  As little skill to fear as I have purpose
  To put you to't. But come, our dance, I pray.
  Your hand, my Perdita: so turtles pair,
  That never mean to part.

PERDITA   I'll swear for 'em.

POLIXENES
  This is the prettiest low-born lass that ever
  Ran on the greensward: nothing she does or seems
  But smacks of something greater than herself,
  Too noble for this place.

CAMILLO   He tells her something
  That makes her blood look out. Good sooth, she is   160
  The queen of curds and cream.

CLOWN Come on, strike up!

DORCAS Mopsa must be your mistress. Marry, garlic to
  mend her kissing with!

MOPSA Now, in good time!

CLOWN Not a word, a word: we stand upon our manners.
  Come, strike up!

  Music. A dance of Shepherds and Shepherdesses

POLIXENES
  Pray, good shepherd, what fair swain is this
  Which dances with your daughter?

SHEPHERD
  They call him Doricles, and boasts himself   170
  To have a worthy feeding; but I have it
  Upon his own report and I believe it:
  He looks like sooth. He says he loves my daughter.
  I think so too; for never gazed the moon
  Upon the water as he'll stand and read,

As 'twere, my daughter's eyes; and, to be plain,
I think there is not half a kiss to choose
Who loves another best.

POLIXENES   She dances featly.

SHEPHERD
So she does anything – though I report it,
180   That should be silent. If young Doricles
Do light upon her, she shall bring him that
Which he not dreams of.

Enter Servant

SERVANT O master, if you did but hear the pedlar at the
door, you would never dance again after a tabor and
pipe; no, the bagpipe could not move you. He sings
several tunes faster than you'll tell money; he utters
them as he had eaten ballads and all men's ears grew to
his tunes.

CLOWN He could never come better; he shall come in. I
190   love a ballad but even too well, if it be doleful matter
merrily set down; or a very pleasant thing indeed, and
sung lamentably.

SERVANT He hath songs for man or woman, of all sizes:
no milliner can so fit his customers with gloves. He has
the prettiest love-songs for maids; so without bawdry,
which is strange; with such delicate burdens of dildos
and fadings, jump her and thump her; and where some
stretch-mouthed rascal would, as it were, mean mischief, and break a foul gap into the matter, he makes the
200   maid to answer, 'Whoop, do me no harm, good man';
puts him off, slights him, with 'Whoop, do me no harm,
good man'.

POLIXENES This is a brave fellow.

CLOWN Believe me, thou talk'st of an admirable conceited
fellow. Has he any unbraided wares?

SERVANT He hath ribbons of all the colours i'th'rainbow;

points more than all the lawyers in Bohemia can
learnedly handle, though they come to him by th'gross;
inkles, caddisses, cambrics, lawns. Why, he sings 'em
over as they were gods or goddesses; you would think a 210
smock were a she-angel, he so chants to the sleevehand
and the work about the square on't.

CLOWN Prithee bring him in, and let him approach singing.

PERDITA Forewarn him that he use no scurrilous words
in's tunes.   *Exit Servant*

CLOWN You have of these pedlars that have more in them
than you'd think, sister.

PERDITA Ay, good brother, or go about to think.

Enter Autolycus, singing

AUTOLYCUS

> Lawn as white as driven snow;   220
> Cypress black as e'er was crow;
> Gloves as sweet as damask roses;
> Masks for faces, and for noses;
> Bugle-bracelet, necklace-amber;
> Perfume for a lady's chamber;
> Golden coifs and stomachers
> For my lads to give their dears;
> Pins and poking-sticks of steel;
> What maids lack from head to heel
> Come buy of me, come, come buy, come buy;   230
> Buy, lads, or else your lasses cry: Come buy.

CLOWN If I were not in love with Mopsa, thou shouldst
take no money of me; but being enthralled as I am, it
will also be the bondage of certain ribbons and gloves.

MOPSA I was promised them against the feast, but they
come not too late now.

DORCAS He hath promised you more than that, or there
be liars.

119

MOPSA He hath paid you all he promised you; may be he
240   has paid you more, which will shame you to give him
again.

CLOWN Is there no manners left among maids? Will they
wear their plackets where they should bear their faces?
Is there not milking-time, when you are going to bed, or
kiln-hole, to whistle of these secrets, but you must be
tittle-tattling before all our guests? 'Tis well they are
whisp'ring. Clamor your tongues, and not a word more.

MOPSA I have done. Come, you promised me a tawdry-
lace and a pair of sweet gloves.

250 CLOWN Have I not told thee how I was cozened by the
way and lost all my money?

AUTOLYCUS And indeed, sir, there are cozeners abroad:
therefore it behoves men to be wary.

CLOWN Fear not thou, man; thou shalt lose nothing here.

AUTOLYCUS I hope so, sir, for I have about me many
parcels of charge.

CLOWN What hast here? Ballads?

MOPSA Pray now, buy some. I love a ballad in print a-life,
for then we are sure they are true.

260 AUTOLYCUS Here's one to a very doleful tune, how a
usurer's wife was brought to bed of twenty money-bags
at a burden, and how she longed to eat adders' heads
and toads carbonadoed.

MOPSA Is it true, think you?

AUROLYCUS Very true, and but a month old.

DORCAS Bless me from marrying a usurer!

AUTOLYCUS Here's the midwife's name to't: one Mistress
Taleporter, and five or six honest wives that were present. Why should I carry lies abroad?

270 MOPSA Pray you now, buy it.

CLOWN Come on, lay it by, and let's first see more ballads; we'll buy the other things anon.

AUTOLYCUS Here's another ballad, of a fish that appeared
upon the coast on Wednesday the fourscore of April,
forty thousand fathom above water, and sung this ballad
against the hard hearts of maids. It was thought she was
a woman, and was turned into a cold fish for she would
not exchange flesh with one that loved her. The ballad
is very pitiful, and as true.

DORCAS Is it true too, think you?   280

AUTOLYCUS Five justices' hands at it, and witnesses more
than my pack will hold.

CLOWN Lay it by too. Another.

AUTOLYCUS This is a merry ballad, but a very pretty one.

MOPSA Let's have some merry ones.

AUTOLYCUS Why, this is a passing merry one, and goes
to the tune of 'Two maids wooing a man'. There's
scarce a maid westward but she sings it; 'tis in request, I
can tell you.

MOPSA We can both sing it. If thou'lt bear a part, thou 290
shalt hear; 'tis in three parts.

DORCAS We had the tune on't a month ago.

AUTOLYCUS I can bear my part: you must know 'tis my
occupation. Have at it with you.

They sing

AUTOLYCUS Get you hence, for I must go.
           Where it fits not you to know.

DORCAS Whither?

MOPSA   O whither?

DORCAS   Whither?

MOPSA It becomes thy oath full well
       Thou to me thy secrets tell.

DORCAS Me too; let me go thither.   300

MOPSA Or thou go'st to th'grange or mill.

DORCAS If to either, thou dost ill.

AUTOLYCUS Neither.

DORCAS	What, neither?
AUTOLYCUS	Neither.
DORCAS	Thou hast sworn my love to be.
MOPSA	Thou hast sworn it more to me.
	Then whither go'st? Say, whither?

CLOWN We'll have this song out anon by ourselves: my
father and the gentlemen are in sad talk, and we'll not
trouble them. Come, bring away thy pack after me.
310 Wenches, I'll buy for you both. Pedlar, let's have the
first choice. Follow me, girls.

Exit with Dorcas and Mopsa

AUTOLYCUS And you shall pay well for 'em.

He follows them, singing
> Will you buy any tape,
> Or lace for your cape,
> My dainty duck, my dear-a?
> Any silk, any thread,
> Any toys for your head,
> Of the new'st and fin'st, fin'st wear-a?
> Come to the pedlar:
320 Money's a meddler
> That doth utter all men's ware-a.   *Exit*

Enter Servant

SERVANT Master, there is three carters, three shepherds,
three neat-herds, three swine-herds, that have made
themselves all men of hair: they call themselves
Saltiers, and they have a dance which the wenches say
is a gallimaufry of gambols, because they are not in't;
but they themselves are o'th'mind, if it be not too rough
for some that know little but bowling it will please
plentifully.

330 SHEPHERD Away! We'll none on't: here has been too
much homely foolery already. I know, sir, we weary you.

POLIXENES You weary those that refresh us. Pray, let's
see these four threes of herdsmen.

SERVANT One three of them, by their own report, sir,
hath danced before the King; and not the worst of the
three but jumps twelve foot and a half by th'square.

SHEPHERD Leave your prating. Since these good men are
pleased, let them come in; but quickly now.

SERVANT Why, they stay at door, sir.

*He lets in the herdsmen, who perform their satyrs'
dance and depart*

POLIXENES (*to Shepherd*)

O, father, you'll know more of that hereafter.   340
(*To Camillo*) Is it not too far gone? 'Tis time to part them.
He's simple and tells much. (*To Florizel*) How now, fair
   shepherd!
Your heart is full of something that does take
Your mind from feasting. Sooth, when I was young
And handed love as you do, I was wont
To load my she with knacks. I would have ransacked
The pedlar's silken treasury, and have poured it
To her acceptance: you have let him go
And nothing marted with him. If your lass
Interpretation should abuse and call this   350
Your lack of love or bounty, you were straited
For a reply, at least if you make a care
Of happy holding her.

FLORIZEL   Old sir, I know
She prizes not such trifles as these are:
The gifts she looks from me are packed and locked
Up in my heart, which I have given already,
But not delivered. O, hear me breathe my life
Before this ancient sir, whom, it should seem,
Hath sometime loved! I take thy hand, this hand
As soft as dove's down and as white as it,   360

123

    Or Ethiopian's tooth, or the fanned snow that's bolted
    By th'northern blasts twice o'er –

POLIXENES   What follows this?
    How prettily the young swain seems to wash
    The hand was fair before! I have put you out.
    But to your protestation: let me hear
    What you profess.

FLORIZEL   Do, and be witness to't.

POLIXENES
    And this my neighbour too?

FLORIZEL   And he, and more
    Than he, and men; the earth, the heavens, and all:
    That were I crowned the most imperial monarch,
370   Thereof most worthy, were I the fairest youth
    That ever made eye swerve, had force and knowledge
    More than was ever man's, I would not prize them
    Without her love; for her employ them all;
    Commend them and condemn them to her service
    Or to their own perdition.

POLIXENES   Fairly offered.

CAMILLO
    This shows a sound affection.

SHEPHERD   But, my daughter,
    Say you the like to him?

PERDITA   I cannot speak
    So well, nothing so well; no, nor mean better.
    By th'pattern of mine own thoughts I cut out
380   The purity of his.

SHEPHERD   Take hands, a bargain!
    And, friends unknown, you shall bear witness to't.
    I give my daughter to him, and will make
    Her portion equal his.

FLORIZEL   O, that must be
    I'th'virtue of your daughter. One being dead,

I shall have more than you can dream of yet;
Enough then for your wonder. But come on:
Contract us 'fore these witnesses.

SHEPHERD   Come, your hand;
And, daughter, yours.

POLIXENES   Soft, swain, awhile, beseech you.
Have you a father?

FLORIZEL   I have; but what of him?

POLIXENES
Knows he of this?

FLORIZEL   He neither does nor shall.   390

POLIXENES
Methinks a father
Is at the nuptial of his son a guest
That best becomes the table. Pray you once more,
Is not your father grown incapable
Of reasonable affairs? Is he not stupid
With age and altering rheums? Can he speak? Hear?
Know man from man? Dispute his own estate?
Lies he not bed-rid? And again does nothing
But what he did being childish?

FLORIZEL   No, good sir:
He has his health, and ampler strength indeed   400
Than most have of his age.

POLIXENES   By my white beard,
You offer him, if this be so, a wrong
Something unfilial. Reason my son
Should choose himself a wife, but as good reason
The father, all whose joy is nothing else
But fair posterity, should hold some counsel
In such a business.

FLORIZEL   I yield all this;
But for some other reasons, my grave sir,
Which 'tis not fit you know, I not acquaint

410 My father of this business.

POLIXENES   Let him know't.

FLORIZEL
  He shall not.

POLIXENES   Prithee, let him.

FLORIZEL   No, he must not.

SHEPHERD
  Let him, my son: he shall not need to grieve
  At knowing of thy choice.

FLORIZEL   Come, come, he must not.
  Mark our contract.

POLIXENES (*removing his disguise*) Mark your divorce, young sir,
  Whom son I dare not call: thou art too base
  To be acknowledged. Thou a sceptre's heir,
  That thus affects a sheep-hook? – Thou, old traitor,
  I am sorry that by hanging thee I can
  But shorten thy life one week. – And thou, fresh piece
420 Of excellent witchcraft, who of force must know
  The royal fool thou cop'st with –

SHEPHERD   O, my heart!

POLIXENES
  I'll have thy beauty scratched with briers and made
  More homely than thy state. – For thee, fond boy,
  If I may ever know thou dost but sigh
  That thou no more shalt see this knack – as never
  I mean thou shalt – we'll bar thee from succession;
  Not hold thee of our blood, no, not our kin,
  Far than Deucalion off. Mark thou my words!
  Follow us to the court. – Thou, churl, for this time,
430 Though full of our displeasure, yet we free thee
  From the dead blow of it. – And you, enchantment,
  Worthy enough a herdsman – yea, him too,
  That makes himself, but for our honour therein,

Unworthy thee – if ever henceforth thou
These rural latches to his entrance open,
Or hoop his body more with thy embraces,
I will devise a death as cruel for thee
As thou art tender to't.   *Exit*

PERDITA   Even here undone!
I was not much afeard; for once or twice
I was about to speak and tell him plainly,   440
The selfsame sun that shines upon his court
Hides not his visage from our cottage, but
Looks on alike. (*To Florizel*) Will't please you, sir, be
    gone?
I told you what would come of this. Beseech you,
Of your own state take care. This dream of mine –
Being now awake, I'll queen it no inch farther,
But milk my ewes, and weep.

CAMILLO   Why, how now, father!
Speak ere thou die'st.

SHEPHERD   I cannot speak nor think,
Nor dare to know that which I know. (*To Florizel*) O sir!
You have undone a man of fourscore three,   450
That thought to fill his grave in quiet, yea,
To die upon the bed my father died,
To lie close by his honest bones; but now
Some hangman must put on my shroud and lay me
Where no priest shovels in dust. (*To Perdita*) O cursed
    wretch,
That knew'st this was the Prince and wouldst adventure
To mingle faith with him! Undone, undone!
If I might die within this hour, I have lived
To die when I desire.   *Exit*

FLORIZEL   Why look you so upon me?
I am but sorry, not afeard; delayed,   460
But nothing altered: what I was I am;

127

More straining on for plucking back, not following
My leash unwillingly.

CAMILLO   Gracious my lord,
You know your father's temper. At this time
He will allow no speech – which I do guess
You do not purpose to him – and as hardly
Will he endure your sight as yet, I fear.
Then till the fury of his highness settle
Come not before him.

FLORIZEL   I not purpose it.

470 I think Camillo?

CAMILLO   Even he, my lord.

PERDITA
How often have I told you 'twould be thus!
How often said my dignity would last
But till 'twere known!

FLORIZEL   It cannot fail but by
The violation of my faith; and then
Let Nature crush the sides o'th'earth together
And mar the seeds within! Lift up thy looks.
From my succession wipe me, father, I
Am heir to my affection.

CAMILLO   Be advised.

FLORIZEL
I am, and by my fancy. If my reason

480 Will thereto be obedient, I have reason;
If not, my senses, better pleased with madness,
Do bid it welcome.

CAMILLO   This is desperate, sir.

FLORIZEL
So call it, but it does fulfil my vow:
I needs must think it honesty. Camillo,
Not for Bohemia, nor the pomp that may
Be thereat gleaned; for all the sun sees or

128

The close earth wombs or the profound seas hides
In unknown fathoms, will I break my oath
To this my fair beloved. Therefore, I pray you,
As you've e'er been my father's honoured friend,   490
When he shall miss me – as, in faith, I mean not
To see him any more – cast your good counsels
Upon his passion. Let myself and Fortune
Tug for the time to come. This you may know,
And so deliver: I am put to sea
With her who here I cannot hold on shore;
And most opportune to our need I have
A vessel rides fast by, but not prepared
For this design. What course I mean to hold
Shall nothing benefit your knowledge, nor   500
Concern me the reporting.

CAMILLO   O my lord,
I would your spirit were easier for advice,
Or stronger for your need.

FLORIZEL   Hark, Perdita –
(to Camillo) I'll hear you by and by.
        He draws Perdita aside

CAMILLO   He's irremovable,
Resolved for flight. Now were I happy if
His going I could frame to serve my turn,
Save him from danger, do him love and honour,
Purchase the sight again of dear Sicilia
And that unhappy king, my master, whom
I so much thirst to see.

FLORIZEL   Now, good Camillo,   510
I am so fraught with curious business that
I leave out ceremony.

CAMILLO   Sir, I think
You have heard of my poor services i'th'love
That I have borne your father?

FLORIZEL   Very nobly
Have you deserved: it is my father's music
To speak your deeds, not little of his care
To have them recompensed as thought on.

CAMILLO   Well, my lord,
If you may please to think I love the King,
And through him what's nearest to him, which is
520 Your gracious self, embrace but my direction.
If your more ponderous and settled project
May suffer alteration, on mine honour,
I'll point you where you shall have such receiving
As shall become your highness: where you may
Enjoy your mistress, from the whom, I see,
There's no disjunction to be made but by –
As heavens forfend! – your ruin; marry her;
And, with my best endeavours in your absence,
Your discontenting father strive to qualify,
530 And bring him up to liking.

FLORIZEL   How, Camillo,
May this, almost a miracle, be done?
That I may call thee something more than man,
And after that trust to thee.

CAMILLO   Have you thought on
A place whereto you'll go?

FLORIZEL   Not any yet:
But as th'unthought-on accident is guilty
To what we wildly do, so we profess
Ourselves to be the slaves of chance, and flies
Of every wind that blows.

CAMILLO   Then list to me.
This follows, if you will not change your purpose
540 But undergo this flight: make for Sicilia,
And there present yourself and your fair princess –
For so I see she must be – 'fore Leontes.

She shall be habited as it becomes
The partner of your bed. Methinks I see
Leontes opening his free arms and weeping
His welcomes forth; asks thee, the son, forgiveness
As 'twere i'th'father's person; kisses the hands
Of your fresh princess; o'er and o'er divides him
'Twixt his unkindness and his kindness: th'one
He chides to hell and bids the other grow   550
Faster than thought or time.

FLORIZEL   Worthy Camillo,
What colour for my visitation shall I
Hold up before him?

CAMILLO   Sent by the King your father
To greet him and to give him comforts. Sir,
The manner of your bearing towards him, with
What you, as from your father, shall deliver –
Things known betwixt us three – I'll write you down,
The which shall point you forth at every sitting
What you must say: that he shall not perceive
But that you have your father's bosom there   560
And speak his very heart.

FLORIZEL   I am bound to you.
There is some sap in this.

CAMILLO   A course more promising
Than a wild dedication of yourselves
To unpathed waters, undreamed shores, most certain
To miseries enough: no hope to help you,
But as you shake off one to take another;
Nothing so certain as your anchors, who
Do their best office if they can but stay you
Where you'll be loath to be. Besides, you know
Prosperity's the very bond of love,   570
Whose fresh complexion and whose heart together
Affliction alters.

131

PERDITA   One of these is true:
I think affliction may subdue the cheek,
But not take in the mind.

CAMILLO   Yea? Say you so?
There shall not at your father's house these seven years
Be born another such.

FLORIZEL   My good Camillo,
She is as forward of her breeding as
She is i'th'rear' our birth.

CAMILLO   I cannot say 'tis pity
She lacks instructions, for she seems a mistress
580 To most that teach.

PERDITA   Your pardon, sir; for this
I'll blush you thanks.

FLORIZEL   My prettiest Perdita!
But O, the thorns we stand upon! Camillo –
Preserver of my father, now of me,
The medicine of our house – how shall we do?
We are not furnished like Bohemia's son,
Nor shall appear in Sicilia.

CAMILLO   My lord,
Fear none of this. I think you know my fortunes
Do all lie there. It shall be so my care
To have you royally appointed as if
590 The scene you play were mine. For instance, sir,
That you may know you shall not want, one word.

They talk aside
Enter Autolycus

AUTOLYCUS Ha, ha, what a fool Honesty is! And Trust,
his sworn brother, a very simple gentleman! I have sold
all my trumpery: not a counterfeit stone, not a ribbon,
glass, pomander, brooch, table-book, ballad, knife, tape,
glove, shoe-tie, bracelet, horn-ring, to keep my pack
from fasting. They throng who should buy first, as if my

trinkets had been hallowed and brought a benediction to
the buyer; by which means I saw whose purse was best
in picture; and what I saw, to my good use I re- 600
membered. My clown, who wants but something to be a
reasonable man, grew so in love with the wenches' song
that he would not stir his pettitoes till he had both tune
and words; which so drew the rest of the herd to me
that all their other senses stuck in ears: you might have
pinched a placket, it was senseless; 'twas nothing to
geld a codpiece of a purse; I would have filed keys off
that hung in chains. No hearing, no feeling, but my sir's
song, and admiring the nothing of it. So that in this time
of lethargy I picked and cut most of their festival 610
purses; and had not the old man come in with a hubbub
against his daughter and the King's son and scared my
choughs from the chaff, I had not left a purse alive in
the whole army.

   Camillo, Florizel, and Perdita come forward

CAMILLO
  Nay, but my letters, by this means being there
  So soon as you arrive, shall clear that doubt.

FLORIZEL
  And those that you'll procure from King Leontes –

CAMILLO
  Shall satisfy your father.

PERDITA   Happy be you!
  All that you speak shows fair.

CAMILLO (*seeing Autolycus*)   Who have we here?
  We'll make an instrument of this, omit   620
  Nothing may give us aid.

AUTOLYCUS (*aside*) If they have overheard me now –
  why, hanging.

CAMILLO How now, good fellow! Why shak'st thou so?
  Fear not, man: here's no harm intended to thee.

AUTOLYCUS I am a poor fellow, sir.

CAMILLO Why, be so still: here's nobody will steal that from thee. Yet for the outside of thy poverty we must make an exchange; therefore discase thee instantly –
630   thou must think there's a necessity in't – and change garments with this gentleman. Though the pennyworth on his side be the worst, yet hold thee, there's some boot.

> *He gives him money*

AUTOLYCUS I am a poor fellow, sir. (*Aside*) I know ye well enough.

CAMILLO Nay, prithee, dispatch. The gentleman is half flayed already.

AUTOLYCUS Are you in earnest, sir? (*Aside*) I smell the trick on't.

640 FLORIZEL Dispatch, I prithee.

AUTOLYCUS Indeed, I have had earnest, but I cannot with conscience take it.

CAMILLO Unbuckle, unbuckle.

> *Florizel and Autolycus exchange garments*

　　　　Fortunate mistress – let my prophecy
Come home to ye! – you must retire yourself
Into some covert; take your sweetheart's hat
And pluck it o'er your brows, muffle your face,
Dismantle you, and, as you can, disliken
The truth of your own seeming, that you may –
650 For I do fear eyes over – to shipboard
Get undescried.

PERDITA　　　　　　　I see the play so lies
That I must bear a part.

CAMILLO　　　　　　　No remedy.
Have you done there?

FLORIZEL　　　　　　　Should I now meet my father,
He would not call me son.

CAMILLO   Nay, you shall have no hat.
   He gives the hat to Perdita
   Come, lady, come. Farewell, my friend.
AUTOLYCUS   Adieu, sir.
FLORIZEL
   O Perdita, what have we twain forgot!
   Pray you, a word.
CAMILLO (*aside*)
   What I do next shall be to tell the King
   Of this escape and whither they are bound;
   Wherein my hope is I shall so prevail   660
   To force him after: in whose company
   I shall re-view Sicilia, for whose sight
   I have a woman's longing.
FLORIZEL   Fortune speed us!
   Thus we set on, Camillo, to th'seaside.
CAMILLO
   The swifter speed the better.
                 Exeunt Florizel, Perdita, and Camillo
AUTOLYCUS I understand the business, I hear it. To have
   an open ear, a quick eye, and a nimble hand is necessary
   for a cutpurse; a good nose is requisite also, to smell out
   work for th'other senses. I see this is the time that the
   unjust man doth thrive. What an exchange had this been   670
   without boot! What a boot is here, with this exchange!
   Sure, the gods do this year connive at us, and we may do
   anything extempore. The Prince himself is about a piece
   of iniquity – stealing away from his father, with his clog
   at his heels. If I thought it were a piece of honesty to
   acquaint the King withal, I would not do't. I hold it the
   more knavery to conceal it; and therein am I constant to
   my profession.
   Enter Clown and Shepherd
   Aside, aside! Here is more matter for a hot brain. Every

680 lane's end, every shop, church, session, hanging, yields
a careful man work.

CLOWN See, see, what a man you are now! There is no
other way but to tell the King she's a changeling and
none of your flesh and blood.

SHEPHERD Nay, but hear me.

CLOWN Nay, but hear me.

SHEPHERD Go to, then.

CLOWN She being none of your flesh and blood, your
flesh and blood has not offended the King; and so your
690 flesh and blood is not to be punished by him. Show
those things you found about her, those secret things,
all but what she has with her. This being done, let the
law go whistle, I warrant you.

SHEPHERD I will·tell the King all, every word – yea, and
his son's pranks too; who, I may say, is no honest man,
neither to his father nor to me, to go about to make me
the King's brother-in-law.

CLOWN Indeed, brother-in-law was the farthest off you
could have been to him; and then your blood had been
700 the dearer by I know not how much an ounce.

AUTOLYCUS (*aside*) Very wisely, puppies!

SHEPHERD Well, let us to the King. There is that in this
fardel will make him scratch his beard.

AUTOLYCUS (*aside*) I know not what impediment this
complaint may be to the flight of my master.

CLOWN Pray heartily he be at palace.

AUTOLYCUS (*aside*) Though I am not naturally honest, I
am so sometimes by chance. Let me pocket up my
pedlar's excrement.

He takes off his false beard

710 How now, rustics! Whither are you bound?

SHEPHERD To th'palace, an it like your worship.

AUTOLYCUS Your affairs there, what, with whom, the

condition of that fardel, the place of your dwelling, your
names, your ages, of what having, breeding, and anything that is fitting to be known, discover.

CLOWN We are but plain fellows, sir.

AUTOLYCUS A lie: you are rough and hairy. Let me have
no lying: it becomes none but tradesmen, and they often
give us soldiers the lie; but we pay them for it with
stamped coin, not stabbing steel; therefore they do not 720
give us the lie.

CLOWN Your worship had like to have given us one, if
you had not taken yourself with the manner.

SHEPHERD Are you a courtier, an't like you, sir?

AUTOLYCUS Whether it like me or no, I am a courtier.
Seest thou not the air of the court in these enfoldings?
Hath not my gait in it the measure of the court? Receives not thy nose court-odour from me? Reflect I not
on thy baseness court-contempt? Think'st thou, for
that I insinuate, to toaze from thee thy business, I am 730
therefore no courtier? I am courtier cap-à-pie; and one
that will either push on or pluck back thy business
there; whereupon I command thee to open thy affair.

SHEPHERD My business, sir, is to the King.

AUTOLYCUS What advocate hast thou to him?

SHEPHERD I know not, an't like you.

CLOWN Advocate's the court-word for a pheasant: say
you have none.

SHEPHERD None, sir; I have no pheasant, cock nor hen.

AUTOLYCUS

How blessed are we that are not simple men!   740
Yet Nature might have made me as these are:
Therefore I'll not disdain.

CLOWN (aside to Shepherd) This cannot be but a great
courtier.

137

SHEPHERD His garments are rich, but he wears them not handsomely.

CLOWN He seems to be the more noble in being fantastical. A great man, I'll warrant. I know by the picking on's teeth.

750 AUTOLYCUS The fardel there, what's i'th'fardel? Wherefore that box?

SHEPHERD Sir, there lies such secrets in this fardel and box, which none must know but the King; and which he shall know within this hour, if I may come to th'speech of him.

AUTOLYCUS Age, thou hast lost thy labour.

SHEPHERD Why, sir?

AUTOLYCUS The King is not at the palace; he is gone aboard a new ship, to purge melancholy and air him-
760 self: for, if thou be'st capable of things serious, thou must know the King is full of grief.

SHEPHERD So 'tis said, sir: about his son, that should have married a shepherd's daughter.

AUTOLYCUS If that shepherd be not in handfast, let him fly: the curses he shall have, the tortures he shall feel, will break the back of man, the heart of monster.

CLOWN Think you so, sir?

AUTOLYCUS Not he alone shall suffer what wit can make heavy and vengeance bitter; but those that are germane
770 to him, though removed fifty times, shall all come under the hangman – which, though it be great pity, yet it is necessary. An old sheep-whistling rogue, a ram-tender, to offer to have his daughter come into grace? Some say he shall be stoned; but that death is too soft for him, say I. Draw our throne into a sheep-cote? All deaths are too few, the sharpest too easy.

CLOWN Has the old man e'er a son, sir, do you hear, an't like you, sir?

AUTOLYCUS He has a son: who shall be flayed alive; then, 'nointed over with honey, set on the head of a 780 wasp's nest; then stand till he be three-quarters and a dram dead; then recovered again with aqua-vitae or some other hot infusion; then, raw as he is, and in the hottest day prognostication proclaims, shall he be set against a brick wall, the sun looking with a southward eye upon him, where he is to behold him with flies blown to death. But what talk we of these traitorly rascals, whose miseries are to be smiled at, their offences being so capital? Tell me, for you seem to be honest, plain men, what you have to the King. Being something 790 gently considered, I'll bring you where he is aboard, tender your persons to his presence, whisper him in your behalfs; and if it be in man besides the King to effect your suits, here is man shall do it.

CLOWN He seems to be of great authority. Close with him, give him gold; and though authority be a stubborn bear, yet he is oft led by the nose with gold. Show the inside of your purse to the outside of his hand, and no more ado. Remember, stoned, and flayed alive!

SHEPHERD An't please you, sir, to undertake the business 800 for us, here is that gold I have. I'll make it as much more, and leave this young man in pawn till I bring it you.

AUTOLYCUS After I have done what I promised?

SHEPHERD Ay, sir.

AUTOLYCUS Well, give me the moiety. (*To the Clown*) Are you a party in this business?

CLOWN In some sort, sir: but though my case be a pitiful one, I hope I shall not be flayed out of it.

AUTOLYCUS O, that's the case of the shepherd's son. 810 Hang him, he'll be made an example.

CLOWN (*aside to Shepherd*) Comfort, good comfort! We

must to the King and show our strange sights. He must
know 'tis none of your daughter, nor my sister; we are
gone else. (*To Autolycus*) Sir, I will give you as much as
this old man does, when the business is performed; and
remain, as he says, your pawn till it be brought you.

AUTOLYCUS I will trust you. Walk before toward the seaside; go on the right hand: I will but look upon the
820 hedge, and follow you.

CLOWN (*aside to Shepherd*) We are blest in this man, as I
may say, even blest.

SHEPHERD Let's before, as he bids us. He was provided
to do us good.   *Exeunt Shepherd and Clown*

AUTOLYCUS If I had a mind to be honest, I see Fortune
would not suffer me: she drops booties in my mouth. I
am courted now with a double occasion: gold, and a
means to do the Prince my master good; which who
knows how that may turn back to my advancement? I
830 will bring these two moles, these blind ones, aboard
him. If he think it fit to shore them again, and that the
complaint they have to the King concerns him nothing,
let him call me rogue for being so far officious; for I am
proof against that title, and what shame else belongs
to't. To him will I present them: there may be matter
in it.   *Exit*

*

V.1   *Enter Leontes, Cleomenes, Dion, Paulina, and others*
CLEOMENES
Sir, you have done enough, and have performed
A saint-like sorrow. No fault could you make
Which you have not redeemed; indeed, paid down
More penitence than done trespass. At the last,

Do as the heavens have done, forget your evil;
With them forgive yourself.

LEONTES   Whilst I remember
Her and her virtues, I cannot forget
My blemishes in them, and so still think of
The wrong I did myself: which was so much
That heirless it hath made my kingdom and   10
Destroyed the sweet'st companion that e'er man
Bred his hopes out of.

PAULINA   True, too true, my lord.
If one by one you wedded all the world,
Or from the all that are took something good
To make a perfect woman, she you killed
Would be unparalleled.

LEONTES   I think so. Killed!
She I killed! I did so; but thou strik'st me
Sorely to say I did. It is as bitter
Upon thy tongue as in my thought. Now, good now,
Say so but seldom.

CLEOMENES   Not at all, good lady.   20
You might have spoken a thousand things that would
Have done the time more benefit and graced
Your kindness better.

PAULINA   You are one of those
Would have him wed again.

DION   If you would not so,
You pity not the state, nor the remembrance
Of his most sovereign name; consider little
What dangers by his highness' fail of issue
May drop upon his kingdom and devour
Incertain lookers-on. What were more holy
Than to rejoice the former queen is well?   30
What holier than, for royalty's repair,
For present comfort and for future good,

    To bless the bed of majesty again
    With a sweet fellow to't?

PAULINA   There is none worthy,
    Respecting her that's gone. Besides the gods
    Will have fulfilled their secret purposes:
    For has not the divine Apollo said,
    Is't not the tenor of his oracle,
    That King Leontes shall not have an heir
40   Till his lost child be found? Which that it shall
    Is all as monstrous to our human reason
    As my Antigonus to break his grave
    And come again to me; who, on my life,
    Did perish with the infant. 'Tis your counsel
    My lord should to the heavens be contrary,
    Oppose against their wills. (*To Leontes*) Care not for
        issue.
    The crown will find an heir. Great Alexander
    Left his to th'worthiest; so his successor
    Was like to be the best.

LEONTES   Good Paulina,
50   Who hast the memory of Hermione,
    I know, in honour, O that ever I
    Had squared me to thy counsel! Then even now
    I might have looked upon my queen's full eyes,
    Have taken treasure from her lips –

PAULINA   And left them
    More rich for what they yielded.

LEONTES   Thou speak'st truth.
    No more such wives, therefore no wife: one worse,
    And better used, would make her sainted spirit
    Again possess her corpse, and on this stage,
    Where we offenders move, appear soul-vexed,
60   And begin, 'Why to me?'

PAULINA   Had she such power,

She had just cause.

LEONTES   She had, and would incense me
To murder her I married.

PAULINA   I should so.
Were I the ghost that walked, I'd bid you mark
Her eye, and tell me for what dull part in't
You chose her; then I'd shriek, that even your ears
Should rift to hear me; and the words that followed
Should be 'Remember mine.'

LEONTES   Stars, stars,
And all eyes else dead coals! Fear thou no wife;
I'll have no wife, Paulina.

PAULINA   Will you swear
Never to marry but by my free leave?   70

LEONTES
Never, Paulina, so be blest my spirit!

PAULINA
Then, good my lords, bear witness to his oath.

CLEOMENES
You tempt him over-much.

PAULINA   Unless another,
As like Hermione as is her picture,
Affront his eye.

CLEOMENES   Good madam –

PAULINA   I have done.
Yet if my lord will marry – if you will, sir,
No remedy, but you will – give me the office
To choose you a queen: she shall not be so young
As was your former, but she shall be such
As, walked your first queen's ghost, it should take joy   80
To see her in your arms.

LEONTES   My true Paulina,
We shall not marry till thou bid'st us.

PAULINA   That

143

Shall be when your first queen's again in breath;
Never till then.

Enter a Gentleman

GENTLEMAN
One that gives out himself Prince Florizel,
Son of Polixenes, with his princess – she
The fairest I have yet beheld – desires access
To your high presence.

LEONTES   What with him? He comes not
Like to his father's greatness. His approach
90 So out of circumstance and sudden tells us
'Tis not a visitation framed, but forced
By need and accident. What train?

GENTLEMAN   But few,
And those but mean.

LEONTES   His princess, say you, with him?

GENTLEMAN
Ay, the most peerless piece of earth, I think,
That e'er the sun shone bright on.

PAULINA   O Hermione,
As every present time doth boast itself
Above a better gone, so must thy grave
Give way to what's seen now. (*To the Gentleman*) Sir,
        you yourself
Have said and writ so – but your writing now
100 Is colder than that theme – she had not been,
Nor was not to be, equalled; thus your verse
Flowed with her beauty once. 'Tis shrewdly ebbed
To say you have seen a better.

GENTLEMAN   Pardon, madam.
The one I have almost forgot – your pardon;
The other, when she has obtained your eye
Will have your tongue too. This is a creature,
Would she begin a sect, might quench the zeal

Of all professors else, make proselytes
Of who she but bid follow.

PAULINA   How? Not women!

GENTLEMAN

Women will love her that she is a woman   110
More worth than any man; men that she is
The rarest of all women.

LEONTES   Go, Cleomenes:
Yourself, assisted with your honoured friends,
Bring them to our embracement.

                Exeunt Cleomenes and others
                   Still, 'tis strange
He thus should steal upon us.

PAULINA   Had our prince,
Jewel of children, seen this hour, he had paired
Well with this lord: there was not full a month
Between their births.

LEONTES

          Prithee, no more! Cease! Thou know'st
He dies to me again when talked of. Sure,
When I shall see this gentleman thy speeches   120
Will bring me to consider that which may
Unfurnish me of reason. They are come.

    Enter Florizel, Perdita, Cleomenes, and others
Your mother was most true to wedlock, Prince:
For she did print your royal father off,
Conceiving you. Were I but twenty-one,
Your father's image is so hit in you,
His very air, that I should call you brother,
As I did him, and speak of something wildly
By us performed before. Most dearly welcome,
And your fair princess – goddess! O! Alas,   130
I lost a couple that 'twixt heaven and earth
Might thus have stood, begetting wonder, as

 You, gracious couple, do. And then I lost –
All mine own folly – the society,
Amity too, of your brave father, whom,
Though bearing misery, I desire my life
Once more to look on him.

FLORIZEL   By his command
Have I here touched Sicilia, and from him
Give you all greetings that a king, at friend,
140 Can send his brother; and but infirmity,
Which waits upon worn times, hath something seized
His wished ability, he had himself
The lands and waters 'twixt your throne and his
Measured to look upon you, whom he loves –
He bade me say so – more than all the sceptres
And those that bear them living.

LEONTES   O my brother –
Good gentleman – the wrongs I have done thee stir
Afresh within me; and these thy offices,
So rarely kind, are as interpreters
150 Of my behindhand slackness! – Welcome hither
As is the spring to th'earth! And hath he too
Exposed this paragon to th'fearful usage,
At least ungentle, of the dreadful Neptune
To greet a man not worth her pains, much less
Th'adventure of her person?

FLORIZEL   Good my lord,
She came from Libya.

LEONTES   Where the warlike Smalus,
That noble, honoured lord, is feared and loved?

FLORIZEL
Most royal sir, from thence; from him whose daughter
His tears proclaimed his, parting with her; thence,
160 A prosperous south wind friendly, we have crossed,
To execute the charge my father gave me

For visiting your highness. My best train
I have from your Sicilian shores dismissed;
Who for Bohemia bend, to signify
Not only my success in Libya, sir,
But my arrival, and my wife's, in safety
Here where we are.

LEONTES   The blessèd gods
Purge all infection from our air whilst you
Do climate here! You have a holy father,
A graceful gentleman, against whose person,   170
So sacred as it is, I have done sin:
For which the heavens, taking angry note,
Have left me issueless; and your father's blessed,
As he from heaven merits it, with you,
Worthy his goodness. What might I have been,
Might I a son and daughter now have looked on,
Such goodly things as you!
        Enter a Lord

LORD   Most noble sir,
That which I shall report will bear no credit,
Were not the proof so nigh. Please you, great sir,
Bohemia greets you from himself by me;   180
Desires you to attach his son, who has –
His dignity and duty both cast off –
Fled from his father, from his hopes, and with
A shepherd's daughter.
LEONTES   Where's Bohemia? Speak.
LORD

Here in your city: I now came from him.
I speak amazèdly, and it becomes
My marvel and my message. To your court
Whiles he was hast'ning – in the chase, it seems,
Of this fair couple – meets he on the way

147

190   The father of this seeming lady, and
Her brother, having both their country quitted
With this young prince.

FLORIZEL   Camillo has betrayed me;
Whose honour and whose honesty till now
Endured all weathers.

LORD   Lay't so to his charge.
He's with the King your father.

LEONTES   Who? Camillo?

LORD
Camillo, sir; I spake with him; who now
Has these poor men in question. Never saw I
Wretches so quake: they kneel, they kiss the earth;
Forswear themselves as often as they speak;
200   Bohemia stops his ears, and threatens them
With divers deaths in death.

PERDITA   O my poor father!
The heaven sets spies upon us, will not have
Our contract celebrated.

LEONTES   You are married?

FLORIZEL
We are not, sir, nor are we like to be.
The stars, I see, will kiss the valleys first:
The odds for high and low's alike.

LEONTES   My lord,
Is this the daughter of a king?

FLORIZEL   She is,
When once she is my wife.

LEONTES
That 'once', I see by your good father's speed,
210   Will come on very slowly. I am sorry,
Most sorry, you have broken from his liking,
Where you were tied in duty; and as sorry
Your choice is not so rich in worth as beauty,

That you might well enjoy her.

FLORIZEL   Dear, look up.
Though Fortune, visible an enemy,
Should chase us, with my father, power no jot
Hath she to change our loves. Beseech you, sir,
Remember since you owed no more to Time
Than I do now. With thought of such affections
Step forth mine advocate: at your request   220
My father will grant precious things as trifles.

LEONTES
Would he do so, I'd beg your precious mistress,
Which he counts but a trifle.

PAULINA   Sir, my liege,
Your eye hath too much youth in't. Not a month
'Fore your queen died she was more worth such gazes
Than what you look on now.

LEONTES   I thought of her
Even in these looks I made. But your petition
Is yet unanswered. I will to your father.
Your honour not o'erthrown by your desires,
I am friend to them and you; upon which errand   230
I now go toward him. Therefore follow me,
And mark what way I make. Come, good my lord.

Exeunt

Enter Autolycus and a Gentleman   V.2

AUTOLYCUS Beseech you, sir, were you present at this
relation?

FIRST GENTLEMAN I was by at the opening of the fardel,
heard the old shepherd deliver the manner how he
found it; whereupon, after a little amazedness, we were
all commanded out of the chamber. Only this methought
I heard the shepherd say: he found the child.

AUTOLYCUS I would most gladly know the issue of it.

FIRST GENTLEMAN I make a broken delivery of the
10   business; but the changes I perceived in the King and
Camillo were very notes of admiration. They seemed
almost, with staring on one another, to tear the cases of
their eyes. There was speech in their dumbness, language in their very gesture. They looked as they had
heard of a world ransomed, or one destroyed. A notable
passion of wonder appeared in them; but the wisest be-
holder that knew no more but seeing could not say if
th'importance were joy or sorrow: but in the extremity
of the one it must needs be.

Enter another Gentleman

20 Here comes a gentleman that haply knows more. The
news, Rogero?

SECOND GENTLEMAN Nothing but bonfires. The oracle
is fulfilled: the King's daughter is found. Such a deal of
wonder is broken out within this hour that ballad-
makers cannot be able to express it.

Enter a third Gentleman

Here comes the Lady Paulina's steward; he can deliver
you more. How goes it now, sir? This news, which is
called true, is so like an old tale that the verity of it is in
strong suspicion. Has the King found his heir?

30 THIRD GENTLEMAN Most true, if ever truth were pregnant by circumstance. That which you hear you'll swear
you see, there is such unity in the proofs: the mantle of
Queen Hermione's; her jewel about the neck of it; the
letters of Antigonus found with it, which they know to
be his character; the majesty of the creature in resemblance of the mother; the affection of nobleness which
nature shows above her breeding, and many other
evidences proclaim her with all certainty to be the King's
daughter. Did you see the meeting of the two kings?

SECOND GENTLEMAN No.

THIRD GENTLEMAN Then have you lost a sight which was to be seen, cannot be spoken of. There might you have beheld one joy crown another, so and in such manner that it seemed sorrow wept to take leave of them: for their joy waded in tears. There was casting up of eyes, holding up of hands, with countenance of such distraction that they were to be known by garment, not by favour. Our king, being ready to leap out of himself for joy of his found daughter, as if that joy were now become a loss cries 'O, thy mother, thy mother!'; then asks Bohemia forgiveness; then embraces his son-in-law; then again worries he his daughter with clipping her; now he thanks the old shepherd, which stands by like a weather-bitten conduit of many kings' reigns. I never heard of such another encounter, which lames report to follow it and undoes description to do it.

SECOND GENTLEMAN What, pray you, became of Antigonus, that carried hence the child?

THIRD GENTLEMAN Like an old tale still, which will have matter to rehearse, though credit be asleep and not an ear open: he was torn to pieces with a bear. This avouches the shepherd's son, who has not only his innocence, which seems much, to justify him, but a handkerchief and rings of his that Paulina knows.

FIRST GENTLEMAN What became of his bark and his followers?

THIRD GENTLEMAN Wracked the same instant of their master's death, and in the view of the shepherd: so that all the instruments which aided to expose the child were even then lost when it was found. But O, the noble combat that 'twixt joy and sorrow was fought in Paulina! She had one eye declined for the loss of her husband, another elevated that the oracle was fulfilled.

She lifted the Princess from the earth, and so locks her in embracing as if she would pin her to her heart, that she might no more be in danger of losing.

FIRST GENTLEMAN The dignity of this act was worth the audience of kings and princes, for by such was it acted.

80 THIRD GENTLEMAN One of the prettiest touches of all, and that which angled for mine eyes – caught the water though not the fish – was when at the relation of the Queen's death, with the manner how she came to't bravely confessed and lamented by the King, how attentiveness wounded his daughter; till, from one sign of dolour to another, she did, with an 'Alas!', I would fain say bleed tears; for I am sure my heart wept blood. Who was most marble there changed colour; some swooned, all sorrowed. If all the world could have seen't, 90 the woe had been universal.

FIRST GENTLEMAN Are they returned to the court?

THIRD GENTLEMAN No: the Princess, hearing of her mother's statue, which is in the keeping of Paulina – a piece many years in doing and now newly performed by that rare Italian master, Julio Romano, who, had he himself eternity and could put breath into his work, would beguile Nature of her custom, so perfectly he is her ape: he so near to Hermione hath done Hermione that they say one would speak to her and stand in hope 100 of answer. Thither with all greediness of affection are they gone, and there they intend to sup.

SECOND GENTLEMAN I thought she had some great matter there in hand, for she hath privately, twice or thrice a day, ever since the death of Hermione, visited that removed house. Shall we thither, and with our company piece the rejoicing?

FIRST GENTLEMAN Who would be thence that has the
benefit of access? Every wink of an eye some new grace
will be born. Our absence makes us unthrifty to our
knowledge. Let's along.   *Exeunt Gentlemen* 110

AUTOLYCUS Now, had I not the dash of my former life
in me, would preferment drop on my head. I brought
the old man and his son aboard the Prince; told him I
heard them talk of a fardel and I know not what: but he
at that time overfond of the shepherd's daughter – so he
then took her to be – who began to be much sea-sick,
and himself little better, extremity of weather continuing, this mystery remained undiscovered. But 'tis
all one to me; for had I been the finder-out of this
secret, it would not have relished among my other dis- 120
credits.

Enter Shepherd and Clown

Here come those I have done good to against my will,
and already appearing in the blossoms of their fortune.

SHEPHERD Come, boy, I am past more children; but thy
sons and daughters will be all gentlemen born.

CLOWN You are well met, sir. You denied to fight with
me this other day because I was no gentleman born.
See you these clothes? Say you see them not and think
me still no gentleman born. You were best say these
robes are not gentlemen born. Give me the lie, do, and 130
try whether I am not now a gentleman born.

AUTOLYCUS I know you are now, sir, a gentleman born.

CLOWN Ay, and have been so any time these four hours.

SHEPHERD And so have I, boy.

CLOWN So you have; but I was a gentleman born before
my father: for the King's son took me by the hand, and
called me brother; and then the two kings called my
father brother; and then the Prince my brother and the

Princess my sister called my father father. And so we
140 wept; and there was the first gentleman-like tears that
ever we shed.

SHEPHERD We may live, son, to shed many more.

CLOWN Ay, or else 'twere hard luck, being in so preposterous estate as we are.

AUTOLYCUS I humbly beseech you, sir, to pardon me all
the faults I have committed to your worship, and to give
me your good report to the Prince my master.

SHEPHERD Prithee, son, do: for we must be gentle, now
we are gentlemen.

150 CLOWN Thou wilt amend thy life?

AUTOLYCUS Ay, an it like your good worship.

CLOWN Give me thy hand. I will swear to the Prince thou
art as honest a true fellow as any is in Bohemia.

SHEPHERD You may say it, but not swear it.

CLOWN Not swear it, now I am a gentleman? Let boors
and franklins say it, I'll swear it.

SHEPHERD How if it be false, son?

CLOWN If it be ne'er so false, a true gentleman may
swear it in the behalf of his friend; and I'll swear to the
160 Prince thou art a tall fellow of thy hands, and that thou
wilt not be drunk; but I know thou art no tall fellow of
thy hands, and that thou wilt be drunk. But I'll swear it,
and I would thou wouldst be a tall fellow of thy hands.

AUTOLYCUS I will prove so, sir, to my power.

CLOWN Ay, by any means prove a tall fellow. If I do not
wonder how thou dar'st venture to be drunk, not being
a tall fellow, trust me not. Hark, the kings and the
princes, our kindred, are going to see the Queen's
picture. Come, follow us: we'll be thy good masters.

Exeunt

Enter Leontes, Polixenes, Florizel, Perdita, Camillo, V.3
Paulina, Lords, and Attendants

LEONTES
O grave and good Paulina, the great comfort
That I have had of thee!

PAULINA   What, sovereign sir,
I did not well, I meant well. All my services
You have paid home: but that you have vouchsafed,
With your crowned brother and these your contracted
Heirs of your kingdoms, my poor house to visit,
It is a surplus of your grace, which never
My life may last to answer.

LEONTES   O Paulina,
We honour you with trouble. But we came
To see the statue of our queen: your gallery   10
Have we passed through, not without much content
In many singularities; but we saw not
That which my daughter came to look upon,
The statue of her mother.

PAULINA   As she lived peerless,
So her dead likeness I do well believe
Excels whatever yet you looked upon,
Or hand of man hath done; therefore I keep it
Lonely, apart. But here it is: prepare
To see the life as lively mocked as ever
Still sleep mocked death. Behold, and say 'tis well!   20
        *Paulina draws a curtain and reveals Hermione, stand-
        ing like a statue*
I like your silence: it the more shows off
Your wonder. But yet speak: first you, my liege.
Comes it not something near?

LEONTES   Her natural posture!
Chide me, dear stone, that I may say indeed
Thou art Hermione; or rather, thou art she

155

In thy not chiding, for she was as tender
As infancy and grace. But yet, Paulina,
Hermione was not so much wrinkled, nothing
So agèd as this seems.

POLIXENES   O, not by much!

PAULINA

30 So much the more our carver's excellence,
Which lets go by some sixteen years and makes her
As she lived now.

LEONTES   As now she might have done,
So much to my good comfort as it is
Now piercing to my soul. O, thus she stood,
Even with such life of majesty – warm life,
As now it coldly stands – when first I wooed her!
I am ashamed. Does not the stone rebuke me
For being more stone than it? O royal piece!
There's magic in thy majesty, which has
40 My evils conjured to remembrance, and
From thy admiring daughter took the spirits,
Standing like stone with thee.

PERDITA   And give me leave,
And do not say 'tis superstition, that
I kneel and then implore her blessing. Lady,
Dear queen, that ended when I but began,
Give me that hand of yours to kiss!

PAULINA   O, patience!
The statue is but newly fixed, the colour's
Not dry.

CAMILLO

My lord, your sorrow was too sore laid on,
50 Which sixteen winters cannot blow away,
So many summers dry. Scarce any joy
Did ever so long live; no sorrow
But killed itself much sooner.

POLIXENES   Dear my brother,
  Let him that was the cause of this have power
  To take off so much grief from you as he
  Will piece up in himself.
PAULINA   Indeed, my lord,
  If I had thought the sight of my poor image
  Would thus have wrought you – for the stone is mine –
  I'd not have showed it.
LEONTES   Do not draw the curtain.
PAULINA
  No longer shall you gaze on't, lest your fancy   60
  May think anon it moves.
LEONTES   Let be, let be!
  Would I were dead but that methinks already –
  What was he that did make it? See, my lord:
  Would you not deem it breathed, and that those veins
  Did verily bear blood?
POLIXENES   Masterly done!
  The very life seems warm upon her lip.
LEONTES
  The fixure of her eye has motion in't
  As we are mocked with art.
PAULINA   I'll draw the curtain.
  My lord's almost so far transported that
  He'll think anon it lives.
LEONTES   O sweet Paulina,   70
  Make me to think so twenty years together!
  No settled senses of the world can match
  The pleasure of that madness. Let't alone.
PAULINA
  I am sorry, sir, I have thus far stirred you; but
  I could afflict you farther.
LEONTES   Do, Paulina:
  For this affliction has a taste as sweet

As any cordial comfort. Still methinks
There is an air comes from her. What fine chisel
Could ever yet cut breath? Let no man mock me,
80   For I will kiss her.

PAULINA   Good my lord, forbear.
The ruddiness upon her lip is wet:
You'll mar it if you kiss it; stain your own
With oily painting. Shall I draw the curtain?

LEONTES
No, not these twenty years.

PERDITA   So long could I
Stand by, a looker-on.

PAULINA   Either forbear,
Quit presently the chapel, or resolve you
For more amazement. If you can behold it,
I'll make the statue move indeed, descend
And take you by the hand: but then you'll think –
90   Which I protest against – I am assisted
By wicked powers.

LEONTES   What you can make her do
I am content to look on; what to speak
I am content to hear; for 'tis as easy
To make her speak as move.

PAULINA   It is required
You do awake your faith. Then all stand still;
Or those that think it is unlawful business
I am about, let them depart.

LEONTES   Proceed.
No foot shall stir.

PAULINA   Music, awake her, strike!
    Music
'Tis time: descend; be stone no more; approach;
100   Strike all that look upon with marvel. Come,
I'll fill your grave up. Stir; nay, come away.

Bequeath to death your numbness, for from him
Dear life redeems you. You perceive she stirs.
   Hermione descends
Start not: her actions shall be holy as
You hear my spell is lawful. (*To Leontes*) Do not shun
     her
Until you see her die again, for then
You kill her double. Nay, present your hand.
When she was young you wooed her: now, in age,
Is she become the suitor?

LEONTES   O, she's warm!
If this be magic, let it be an art   110
Lawful as eating.

POLIXENES   She embraces him.

CAMILLO
She hangs about his neck.
If she pertain to life, let her speak too.

POLIXENES
Ay, and make it manifest where she has lived,
Or how stol'n from the dead.

PAULINA   That she is living,
Were it but told you, should be hooted at
Like an old tale: but it appears she lives,
Though yet she speak not. Mark a little while.
(*To Perdita*) Please you to interpose, fair madam; kneel,
And pray your mother's blessing. Turn, good lady: 120
Our Perdita is found.

HERMIONE   You gods, look down,
And from your sacred vials pour your graces
Upon my daughter's head! Tell me, mine own,
Where hast thou been preserved? Where lived? How
     found
Thy father's court? For thou shalt hear that I,
Knowing by Paulina that the oracle

Gave hope thou wast in being, have preserved
Myself to see the issue.

PAULINA   There's time enough for that,
Lest they desire upon this push to trouble
130 Your joys with like relation. Go together,
You precious winners all; your exultation
Partake to everyone. I, an old turtle,
Will wing me to some withered bough, and there
My mate, that's never to be found again,
Lament till I am lost.

LEONTES   O peace, Paulina!
Thou shouldst a husband take by my consent,
As I by thine a wife. This is a match,
And made between's by vows. Thou hast found mine –
But how is to be questioned: for I saw her,
140 As I thought, dead; and have in vain said many
A prayer upon her grave. I'll not seek far –
For him, I partly know his mind – to find thee
An honourable husband. Come, Camillo,
And take her by the hand; whose worth and honesty
Is richly noted, and here justified
By us, a pair of kings. Let's from this place.
(*To Hermione*) What! Look upon my brother. Both your
    pardons
That e'er I put between your holy looks
My ill suspicion. This' your son-in-law,
150 And son unto the King, whom heavens directing,
Is troth-plight to your daughter. Good Paulina,
Lead us from hence, where we may leisurely
Each one demand and answer to his part
Performed in this wide gap of time since first
We were dissevered. Hastily lead away.

                                        Exeunt

COMMENTARY

THE Act and scene division is that found in the first Folio. In the Commentary and the Account of the Text that edition is usually referred to as F. The quotations from *Pandosto* in both Introduction and Commentary are taken from J. H. P. Pafford's new Arden edition of *The Winter's Tale*, which reprints the text of the 1595 edition of *Pandosto* in a modernized form. Spelling and punctuation in quotations from the writings of Shakespeare's contemporaries have also been modernized.

The Characters in the Play
For the derivation of the names see Introduction, page 11, and notes on III.3.32; IV.1.22; IV.3. 24; IV.4.54; V.1.156.

I.1   (stage direction) *Enter Camillo and Archidamus.* The scene headings throughout the Folio text are silent about the location of each scene. This can, however, be usually inferred from its opening lines, for, in the absence of naturalistic sets, Shakespeare took pains to inform his audience of the scene's approximate location whenever such knowledge is wanted. However, a precise localization (attempted by many later editors) is often impossible, as well as undesirable.

6   *Bohemia* (the King of Bohemia, Polixenes)

9   *justified* acquitted, absolved (of the sin of entertaining you unworthily – a glance at the doctrine of salvation by faith rather than by good works)

11–12   *in the freedom of my knowledge* as my knowledge gives me the right to do

13   *sleepy* inducing sleep

14   *unintelligent* unaware

21-2   *Sicilia ... Bohemia* (the King of Sicilia ... the King of Bohemia)

22-4   *They were trained together in their childhoods; and there rooted betwixt them then such an affection, which cannot choose but branch now.* The horticultural meaning of *trained* is responsible for the metaphors in the remainder of the sentence.

27   *hath* (an instance of the third person plural in 'th') *attorneyed* performed by substitutes

29   *vast* wide expanse

35   *into my note* under my notice

37   *physics the subject* acts as a tonic to the nation

I.2.1-3   *Nine changes of the watery star hath been | The shepherd's note since we have left our throne | Without a burden.* Polixenes has been the guest of Leontes for nine months, time enough to make it possible for him to be Perdita's father.

1   *watery star* (the moon)

3-9   *Time as long ... before it* I ought to spend another nine months thanking you, and yet would depart for ever in your debt; and so one final expression of thanks must multiply all those that preceded it, just as a nought at the end of a number multiplies it, though by itself it is without value

11   *I am questioned by my fears of what may chance* my fears raise questions in me as to what may be happening

12-14   *That may blow | No sneaping winds at home, to make us say | 'This is put forth too truly'!* This passage has been much discussed, but its general meaning is clear enough. Though in F *that* is preceded by a comma, it is probably a wish: 'O, that no sneaping winds may blow at home, to make me say "my fears were only too well grounded!"'

13   *sneaping* nipping, biting

16 *Than you can put us to't* than to be taxed beyond our
    strength by you

17 *sev'n-night* week
    Very sooth truly

18 *between's* between us

19 *I'll no gainsaying* I will not be refused

25 *Were, in your love, a whip to me* would be a punishment
    to me, though you acted out of love

31-2 *this satisfaction | The by-gone day proclaimed* we heard
    this good news yesterday

33 *ward* defensive posture (in fencing)

37 (stage direction) *Leontes draws apart.* This seems the
    most probable moment for the withdrawal of Leontes.
    Up to this point Hermione has been addressing her
    words to him, speaking of Polixenes in the third per-
    son. Now Leontes withdraws and the remainder of the
    speech is addressed directly to Polixenes. Her *yet, good
    deed, Leontes, | I love thee not a jar o'th'clock behind |
    What lady she her lord* would then be spoken to herself,
    out of his hearing. This hypothesis is supported by the
    fact that, whenever elsewhere in the play Hermione
    addresses her husband, she calls him 'sir', 'my lord',
    'your highness', but never 'Leontes'.

40 *take.* Probably the meaning here is 'receive', rather
    than 'charm', 'delight', as some commentators explain
    it.

41 *let him* allow him (to stay)
    gest (a stage of a royal progress, hence the time allotted
    for such a stage)

42 *for's* for his
    good deed indeed, in very truth

43 *jar* tick

44 *What lady she her lord* than any lady whatsoever loves
    her husband

47 *limber* limp, flabby

53-4 *so you shall pay your fees | When you depart.* Prisoners
    in Shakespeare's day were liable to pay fees to the

gaoler upon being freed.

57   *should import offending* should imply that I had committed some offence against you

63   *behind* to follow

68   *changed* exchanged

74-5 *the imposition cleared | Hereditary ours.* A latinism: 'assuming the inherited guilt which is imposed upon us (original sin) to be set aside'. A possible, but much less likely, alternative explanation – favoured by several commentators – makes Polixenes affirm that their boyhood innocence even cleared them of the taint of original sin.

80   *Grace to boot!* Heaven help us!

81   *Of this make no conclusion* do not pursue this argument to a logical conclusion

92-3 *One good deed dying tongueless | Slaughters a thousand waiting upon that* the absence of praise for one good deed leads to the destruction of a thousand others which were ready to be performed

96   *heat an acre* race over a single furlong

99   *Grace.* The primary meaning here is probably that of 'seemliness', 'becomingness', with an intentional pun on the female name.

104   *clap thyself my love* (offer the handclasp that seals the bargain, as was customary at betrothals)

109   *To mingle friendship far is mingling bloods.* In Aristotelian physiology sexual intercourse was thought of as a mingling of bloods (compare Donne's *The Progress of the Soul*, stanza L: 'Adam and Eve had mingled bloods').

110   *tremor cordis* palpitation of the heart

112-13 *May a free face put on, derive a liberty | From heartiness, from bounty, fertile bosom* may wear the look of innocence, may derive a freedom from cordiality, from generosity, from abundance of affection

112   *put on* wear (without any suggestion of deceit)

115   *But to be paddling palms and pinching fingers.* That a

lady's paddling with the palm of a gentleman's hand could be seen both as an accepted form of polite behaviour and as a sign of lasciviousness is illustrated by the conversation between Iago and Roderigo about Desdemona's bearing towards Cassio (*Othello*, II.1. 246–50):

IAGO ... Didst thou not see her paddle with the palm of his hand? Didst not mark that?

RODERIGO Yes, that I did; but that was but courtesy.

IAGO Lechery, by this hand: an index and obscure prologue to the history of lust and foul thoughts.

115 *paddling* fondly fingering

116 *practised* studied

118 *mort o'th'deer*. This is a hunting phrase, denoting the four notes blown to announce the death of the deer. The long-drawn breath needed to blow this could be compared with a sigh. But it is much more likely that the reference is to the dying deer's last sighs, possibly with a pun on *deer*.

119 *nor my brows*. Here and in lines 124–9, 137, 146, and 186 the reference is to the popular jest that horns grow on the forehead of cuckolds.

120 *I'fecks!* (a corruption of 'in faith')

121 *bawcock* fine fellow (from French *beau coq*; a colloquial term of endearment)

123 *not neat but cleanly*. Recollecting that *neat* also means 'horned cattle', Leontes corrects himself.

125 *virginalling* playing with her fingers as if upon the virginals

126 *wanton* frisky, frolicsome

128 *a rough pash and the shoots* a bull's shaggy head and horns

132 *o'er-dyed blacks* (probably blacks (mourning) dyed over in another colour, so that the suggestion not only of falseness in the colour of the garments but also of infidelity in their wearer is involved)

134 *bourn* boundary

136   *welkin* blue as the sky

137   *collop* slice of meat (hence 'my flesh and blood')

        dam mother (part of the cluster of cattle-images set
        off by the allusion to the cuckold's horns in line
        119)

138–46 *Affection, thy intention stabs the centre | . . . of my brows.*
        The meaning of these lines, which have been called
        'the obscurest passage in Shakespeare', has been end-
        lessly discussed. The chief point at issue is whether
        Leontes is speaking of his own feelings or of Her-
        mione's. One group of commentators thinks that
        Leontes is analysing the nature of sexual jealousy and
        that he is saying: 'The feeling of jealousy is often
        based on mere figments; all the more reason, then, that
        it may also join with something real, as it does in my
        case.' But this train of thought lacks logic and does not
        link up well with the immediately preceding words,
        Can thy dam? May't be? Above all the word *affection*
        would be oddly chosen to signify passionate jealousy.
        Its meaning here seems to be rather that of 'sexual
        desire' (as in *The Rape of Lucrece*, line 271). To his
        own question, whether it is possible that Hermione is
        an adulteress, Leontes replies: 'Yes, for sexual desire,
        in its intensity, stabs men to their very soul. It makes
        possible what is else thought impossible, creating an
        imaginary world of wish-fulfilment in dreams. All the
        more credible is it then that it will fasten on a real
        object, and this it does in Hermione's passion for
        Polixenes, which has maddened me and made me a
        cuckold.' The logical train of thought is interrupted by
        how can this be? in line 140, which seems to be a return
        to the opening question, *Can thy dam? May't be?* In
        the very process of being given a reasoned answer, the
        question reasserts itself in Leontes's mind.

138   *Affection* sexual desire
        intention intensity
        centre soul, heart

142   *credent* credible

144   *commission* warrant

146   *What means Sicilia?* This is surely an inquiry not about what Leontes means but about the meaning of his distracted appearance. There is therefore no need or warrant for assuming that any part of his preceding speech is overheard by Hermione and Polixenes.

147   *something* somewhat

148   *What cheer? How is't with you, best brother?* In all the Folios this line is given to Leontes. But the phrase *How is't with you*, which with Shakespeare always has the meaning of 'Are you feeling well?', makes it highly probable that it is spoken by Polixenes.

150   *moved* angered

151   *Nature* the bonds of affection between parents and children

152–3   *a pastime | To harder bosoms* a diversion for those less tender-hearted

154   *methoughts* (a not uncommon variant of 'methought') *recoil* go back in memory

155   *Twenty-three years.* This fixes the age of Leontes in the first half of the play at around thirty. *unbreeched* not yet in breeches

160   *squash* unripe pea-pod

161   *Will you take eggs for money?* (a proverbial expression, meaning 'Will you allow yourself to be fobbed off with something of little value?')

163   *happy man be's dole!* (a common expression, meaning 'May it be his lot in life to be a happy man!')

165   *If at home* when I am at home

166   *all my exercise, my mirth, my matter* that which constantly occupies my attention, the subject of my merry and my serious moments

171   *thick my blood* make me melancholy

171–2   *So stands this squire | Officed with me* just such a part is played by this boy in my household (alluding to the services of squires in royal households)

174-5   *How thou lov'st us show in our brother's welcome. | Let what is dear in Sicily be cheap.* The double meaning of these lines is most probably intended by Leontes.

177   *Apparent to my heart* heir to my affection

178   *Shall's attend you there?* shall we await you there?

182   *Go to, go to!* (an interjection expressing remonstrance or disgust)

183   *neb* beak, mouth

185   *To her allowing husband* towards her husband, who licenses such behaviour

186   *forked one* (an allusion to the cuckold's horns)

187-9   *thy mother plays, and I | Play too – but so disgraced a part, whose issue | Will hiss me to my grave* your mother engages in love-play, and I, too, am playing (namely, the role of a husband who simulates amity towards his unfaithful wife and her lover), but a most shameful part, as the result of which I shall be hissed until the end of my days

189   *Contempt and clamour* (probably a hendiadys: 'an outcry of contempt')

194   *sluiced.* This metaphor, derived from the action of drawing off water from a pond or lake by means of a sluice, leads on to those of the pond and the gates in the succeeding lines.

199   *revolted* unfaithful

201-2   *It is a bawdy planet, that will strike | Where 'tis predominant* it is like a bawdy planet, which will spread ruin whenever it is in the ascendant (the allusion is to the planet Venus). *Strike* ('destroy by malign influence') and *predominant* ('in the ascendant') are both technical terms in astrology.

202   *think it* be assured of it

204   *No barricado for a belly* there is no way of barricading a womb

   Know't be certain of it

206   *on's* of us

208   *I am like you, they say.* This emendation of F's *I am like you say* is found for the first time in the second Folio (1632). An alternative emendation would be 'I am like you, you say'. But though the omission of a second 'you' would be a more likely printer's or copyist's error, *they say* seems the more attractive reading and has been adopted by all editors.

210   (stage direction) *He comes forward.* It must be assumed that up to this point Camillo has hovered at the back of the stage but within hearing of the dialogue.

214   *still came home* always came back

217   *They're here with me already* people are already aware of my situation

218   *Sicilia is a so-forth* the King is a so-and-so (avoiding the open use of 'cuckold')

219   *gust* taste (hence 'know of')

222   *so it is* as things are
         taken comprehended

224   *thy conceit is soaking* your faculty of apprehension is quick to absorb

225   *blocks* blockheads

226   *But of the finer natures* except by the keener minds

227   *Lower messes* inferior people (a 'mess' being a group of people who were served together at table)

228   *purblind* quite blind

233   *Satisfy?* Leontes takes the word in its erotic sense.

236–7   *as well | My chamber-counsels* and also with my intimate confidences (it is unwarrantable to assume that this must refer to sexual transgressions)

242   *bide* insist

244   *Which hoxes honesty behind* which hamstrings honesty (the unusual metaphor, derived from the laming of cattle by cutting their hamstrings, was probably suggested by the popular derivation of 'coward' from 'cowherd')

245–7   *Or else ... or else* either ... or

248   *played home, the rich stake drawn* played to the finish, the high stake taken up by the winner (probably with a bawdy quibble on *the rich stake drawn*)

254   *puts forth* shows itself

256   *industriously* intentionally (corresponding to *wilful* in the previous clause)

260–61   *Whereof the execution did cry out | Against the non-performance* (probably 'the carrying out of which showed how wrong it would have been not to have done it')

263   *that* as

268   *eye-glass* lens of the eye

270   *to a vision so apparent* about something which can be seen so clearly

273   *slippery* unchaste

274–5   *Or else be impudently negative | To have nor eyes, nor ears, nor thought* otherwise you must boldly deny that you can see, hear, and think

276   *hobby-horse* light woman

277   *puts to* goes to it, fornicates

278   *justify* affirm

281   *present* immediate

       'Shrew beshrew

283–4   *which to reiterate were sin | As deep as that, though true.* Commentators agree in making *As deep as that* refer to Hermione's adultery. But it makes much better sense if we take it to refer to the sin committed by Leontes in unjustly accusing her.

286   *career* (literally 'short gallop at full speed', hence 'course')

288   *honesty* chastity

       Horsing foot on foot setting one's foot upon that of the other person (this apparently unique use of the word *horsing* was presumably sparked off by the equestrian metaphor in line 286)

291   *pin and web* (a disease of the eye)

302   *hovering* wavering

306   *The running of one glass* the time it takes for the sand in the hour-glass to run out

307   *like her medal* like a miniature portrait of herself (worn in a locket around the neck)

311   *thrifts* gains

313   *form* rank, quality

314   *benched and reared to worship* given a position of authority and raised to a place of honour

317   *To give mine enemy a lasting wink* to close my enemy's eyes for ever

318   *cordial* restorative, reviving

319   *rash* operating quickly

321   *Maliciously* virulently

322   *crack* flaw

323   *So sovereignly being* being so supremely

324   *I have loved thee.* The use of *thee*, unusual in a subject towards his sovereign, has led some editors to transfer these words to Leontes, or to emend them. But Camillo's special role as the King's intimate and confessor (lines 235–9) sufficiently justifies its use.

       Make that thy question, and go rot! This is a reply to Camillo's expression of disbelief in Hermione's guilt, not to his last words, which Leontes interrupts. 'If you doubt that, go to blazes!'

326   *To appoint my self in this vexation* (probably 'to ordain this affliction for my own self'; the main stress is on *self*)

333   *blench* swerve (from the path of right conduct)

334   *fetch off* do away with, kill. Camillo's choice of this uncommon expression, and again of *removed* in the next line, may be due to his wish to equivocate in order to avoid lying to Leontes, for the common Shakespearian meaning of 'fetch off' is 'rescue', an action which Camillo may be already contemplating. The formulation of his promise in lines 346–7 may be due to the same desire to equivocate, Camillo declaring thus covertly his resolution to leave the service of Leontes.

337 *forsealing*. F's *for sealing* can be made to yield adequate sense if taken to mean 'for the sake of sealing', but this entails a very awkward and un-Shakespearian construction. It seems highly probable that *for* here is an intensive prefix, the word meaning 'sealing up close'.

339-41 *Thou dost advise me | Even so as I mine own course have set down. | I'll give no blemish to her honour, none.* A marked contrast with Pandosto, who intends from the outset 'as soon as Egistus was dead to give his wife a sop of the same sauce, and so be rid of those which were the cause of his restless sorrow' (page 187). In the play it is only the flight of Polixenes and his conviction that Hermione was accessary to it and to a plot against his life that move Leontes to denounce her publicly and to seek her death. It is one of many ways in which Shakespeare makes him more sympathetic than Pandosto.

350 *I will seem friendly, as thou hast advised me.* Leontes does not, in fact, succeed in dissimulating his feelings.

355-6 *Who, in rebellion with himself, will have | All that are his so too* who, being in rebellion against his true and worthy self, wants all his subjects to follow him in this

356 *To do* if I do. This use of the infinitive in a gerundive sense is common with Shakespeare.

362-3 *certain | To me a break-neck* my certain ruin

365 *warp* shrink, shrivel

367 *None rare* nothing unusual

372-3 *Wafting his eyes to th'contrary, and falling| A lip of much contempt* looking the other way, and dropping his lip contemptuously

374 *breeding* afoot

377-80 *How, dare not? Do not? Do you know and dare not | Be intelligent to me? 'Tis thereabouts; | For to yourself what you do know you must, | And cannot say you dare not* how do you mean, dare not? Is it that you *do* not know? Or can it be that you do know but dare not communicate your knowledge to *me*? That must be it:

for you cannot be saying that you don't dare to communicate it to *yourself*

381   *complexions* looks (those of Leontes and Camillo)

382–4 *for I must be | A party in this alteration, finding | Myself*
       thus altered with't for my looks, too, must have
       changed, reflecting the altered position in which I find
       myself

383   *party* participant

388   *Make me not sighted like the basilisk* do not make me out
       to have a gaze like that of the basilisk (a fabulous
       reptile, half cock and half serpent, supposed to be able
       to kill by its look)

392   *Clerk-like experienced* proved to be a man of learning

394   *In whose success we are gentle* in succession from whom
       we are noble

397   *ignorant concealment* concealment that keeps one in
       ignorance

400–   *I conjure thee, by all the parts of man | Which honour*
402   *does acknowledge, whereof the least | Is not this suit of*
       mine I appeal solemnly to you by all the obligations
       which honourable men recognize, not the least of
       which is to answer this request of mine

403   *incidency* event liable to happen

410–11 *or both yourself and me | Cry lost, and so good night* or
       proclaim both yourself and me as lost, and so farewell
       for ever

412   *him* the man

416   *vice* force, constrain (as by the use of a vice)

419   *the Best* Jesus

421   *savour* stench

424   *Swear his thought over* though you should over-swear
       (swear the contrary of) his thought

426   *influences* (a technical term in astrology, designating
       the emanation from the stars, which was believed to
       affect all life on earth)

427   *for to* to

428   *or . . . or* either . . . or

429–31   *whose foundation | Is piled upon his faith, and will continue | The standing of his body* the foundation of which is firmly erected upon his settled belief, and which will last as long as his life

431   *How should this grow?* how should this suspicion have arisen?

435   *this trunk* this body of mine (with a quibble on *trunk* meaning 'coffer')

436   *impawned* as a pledge of my good faith

438   *posterns* back gates in the city walls

441   *discovery* disclosure

448   *places* dignities

449   *Still* always

456   *Professed* made professions of friendship

458–60   *Good expedition be my friend and comfort | The gracious Queen, part of his theme, but nothing | Of his ill-ta'en suspicion!* This passage has been much discussed and emended. It has even been remarked that 'Shakespeare himself *might* be able to tell us what he meant when he wrote it; no one else.' The perplexities are dispelled once we realize (1) that *expedition* here means not 'hasty departure' but 'the action of expediting': this same hastening which Polixenes prays to be his friend, since it will convey him into safety, he also hopes will bring comfort to the Queen by quickly putting an end to the King's suspicions; (2) that *nothing | Of his ill-ta'en suspicion* does not mean that Hermione is not *included* in her husband's wrongly conceived suspicions, but that she does not deserve them, though she is part of his *theme* (which here has the meaning of 'matter for feeling and action').

462   *Hence! Let us avoid* away! let us be gone (many editors adopt the tamer but quite possible reading 'Thou bear'st my life off hence. Let us avoid'. F reads *Thou bear'st my life off, hence: Let vs auoid*.)

I.1. 1–32   This episode is developed from a single line in *Pandosto*, telling how the guards, sent to carry her to prison, 'coming to the queen's lodging ... found her playing with her young son Garinter' (page 190).

3   *I'll none of you* I will have nothing to do with you

9   *so that* provided that

11   *taught'* taught you (the apostrophe, found in F, shows that, for metrical reasons, a word has been omitted)

18   *wanton* sport, play

20   *Good time* a happy issue

27–8   *Come on, sit down; come on, and do your best | To fright me with your sprites*. A poignant touch of dramatic irony: Hermione, still happy and unsuspecting, plays at being frightened by the imaginings of her son, unaware that a few moments later she will be truly frightened by the imaginings of her husband (note also the echo of the words at III.2.91, *The bug which you would fright me with I seek*).

31   *Yond crickets* (a reference to the merry chatter of the ladies-in-waiting)

35   *scour* hurry along

37   *censure* judgement

38   *Alack, for lesser knowledge!* O that I knew less!

39–45   *There may be in the cup | ... seen the spider*. The spider was believed to be venomous and to poison any liquid in which it was found. The superstition referred to here is that its poison operated only if the person consuming the drink was aware of the spider's presence. The analogy is therefore a precise one, reminiscent of a metaphysical conceit.

45   *hefts* retchings

48   *All's true that is mistrusted* all one's suspicions prove to be true

50   *discovered* revealed

51   *pinched*. Various meanings of the word, such as 'tormented', 'reduced to straits', and 'shrunk', may be

involved. This last meaning seems to have led on to
the image in the next sentence.

51   *trick* toy, plaything

52   *play* play with

62   *But I'd say* I should merely have to say

64   *to th'nayward* towards denial

68   *honest* chaste

69   *without-door form* external appearance

72   *I am out!* I am wrong

79   *replenished* complete

82-3   *O thou thing | Which I'll not call a creature of thy place.*
Leontes will not call a person of Hermione's exalted
position by the name she deserves.

85   *degrees* ranks of society

90   *fedary* confederate. F's *Federarie* is most probably a
misprint, since there is no other recorded use of that
word. Both the requirements of metre and Shakespeare's usage elsewhere indicate that he wrote *fedary*.

92   *But with her most vile principal* (probably 'even if no
one except Polixenes were to share that knowledge')
principal person directly responsible for a crime

93   *bed-swerver* adulteress

94   *That vulgars give bold'st titles* to whom the common
people give the coarsest names

98   *published* publicly denounced

102   *centre* the earth (believed to be the centre of the uni-
verse)

104-5   *is afar off guilty | But that he speaks* makes himself in
some measure guilty by merely speaking

107   *aspect* (a technical term in astrology, denoting the way
in which the planets look upon each other; the accent
falls on the second syllable)

111   *honourable* honest

113   *so qualified* of such a nature

118   *good fools* (a term of endearment)

121   *come out* leave the prison

This action I now go on. The word *action* has been ex-

plained by some as meaning 'indictment', which fits
the context but does not suit with *go on*; by others as
meaning 'military operation', which suits with *go on*
but does not fit the context (the notion that Hermione
announces that she is undertaking a campaign for her
honour seems highly implausible). Perhaps the metaphor, like so many in the play, is theatrical, *action* meaning 'the acting of plays': 'the part I now have to play'.

122   *my better grace* my greater credit

134-5   *I'll keep my stables where | I lodge my wife.* The thought
of this much debated passage, though highly con-
densed, is plain enough: if the Queen is unchaste,
Antigonus is saying, then all other women are mere
animals, and I shall treat my wife as such, turning her
chamber into stables, where I shall guard her as strictly
as one does one's mares.

135   *in couples with her* coupled by a leash to her

141   *putter-on* instigator

143   *lam-damn.* After more than two centuries of debate,
commentators are still uncertain of the word's meaning. Of the many proposed emendations – all of them
unconvincing – the most grotesque are Farmer's 'I
would laudanum him' and Schmidt's 'I would – Lord,
damn him!'. In the form 'landam' it has been claimed
to be a Gloucestershire dialect-word, meaning 'to
abuse with rancour' or 'to damn through the land'; in
the form 'lan-dan' it is said to describe a folk-custom
in which the name of a slanderer is publicly proclaimed.
It seems, however, quite possible that it is a nonce-
word, made up by Antigonus from the *damn* of the
preceding line and the verb 'to lam' ('to thrash'), and
that he is saying 'I would thrash him unmercifully'.
If Shakespeare wrote 'lam' as 'lame', it could easily
have been misread as 'land', leading to F's spelling
Land-damne.

145   *The second and the third nine and some five* the second
nine and the third around five

148 *bring false generations* have illegitimate children (in contrast to *fair* ('legitimate') *issue* in line 150)
They are co-heirs. With daughters the law of primogeniture does not operate, so they are joint heirs.

149 *glib* geld

153-4 *As you feel doing thus and see withal | The instruments that feel.* Most commentators think that Leontes at this point pulls Antigonus's beard or tweaks his nose. But *doing thus* without a preceding 'my' and the use of *feel* in line 154 suggest that *you* is here used generically, and that Leontes is striking against a wall or chair with his fingers, which can then fitly be called *The instruments that feel*, without giving to *feel* the rather forced meaning of 'touch'.

157 *dungy* base
Lack I credit? am I not believed?

159 *Upon this ground* in this matter

164 *Calls not* does not call for

165-7 *which, if you – or stupefied | Or seeming so in skill – cannot or will not | Relish a truth like us* (a loose construction, with both *which* and *a truth* as objects of *relish*)

165-6 *or stupefied | Or seeming so in skill* either grown insensible or cunningly pretending to be so

167 *Relish* appreciate

172 *overture* disclosure

175 *familiarity* (to make the line scan the word must here be given six syllables)

176-7 *as gross as ever touched conjecture | That lacked sight only* as palpable as surmise that lacked only actual sight ever reached to

177 *approbation* proof

179 *Made up* added up

182 *wild* rash

182-7 *I have dispatched in post | . . . Shall stop or spur me.* In *Pandosto* the Queen begs her husband 'to send six of his noblemen whom he best trusted to the Isle of Delphos, there to inquire of the oracle of Apollo whether she had committed adultery with Egistus' (page 195). By making the idea of consulting the oracle originate with Leontes, not the Queen, Shakespeare contrived to make him much more sympathetic than Pandosto.

182   *in post* in haste

183   *Delphos*. The island of Delos, the birthplace of Apollo, which also possessed an oracle, was commonly known in Shakespeare's day as 'Delphos'. The fact that Delphi, with its more famous oracle, was also generally called 'Delphos' led to a frequent confusion of the two.

185   *Of stuffed sufficiency* fully qualified for the office

186   *all* the whole truth
      had when received

191   *such as he* (referring to Antigonus)

195   *the treachery of the two fled hence* (the supposed plan to murder Leontes, mentioned by him in lines 47 and 89)

198   *raise* rouse

I.2. 14   *put apart* dismiss

20   *As passes colouring*. Paulina seems to be playing with two meanings of *colouring*: (1) 'dying' ('as exceeds the dyer's art'); (2) 'excusing' ('as passes all excuse').

23   *On* in consequence of

24   *Which* than which

30   *lunes* mad freaks

33   *let my tongue blister*. The reference is to the notion that the utterance of falsehood blisters the tongue.

34-5   *to my red looked anger be | The trumpet*. The trumpeter, on the field of battle, preceded the herald, who was generally dressed in red and often bore angry messages.

39   *advocate to th'loud'st* loudest advocate

44   *free* magnanimous

45   *thriving issue* successful outcome

47   *presently* at once
49   *hammered of* deliberated upon
50   *tempt* make trial of
52   *wit* words of wisdom or good sense
57   *to pass it* by letting it pass

II.3   (stage direction) *Enter Leontes.* Most editors, misled by F's massed entry, *Enter Leontes, Seruants, Paulina, Antigonus, and Lords*, make Leontes enter accompanied by Antigonus, Lords, and Servants, who presumably remain in the background while Leontes soliloquizes. But his *Who's there?* (line 9) and *Leave me solely* (line 17) indicate that he enters alone and that Antigonus, Lords, and Servants do not come in until line 26, when trying to hold back Paulina.

3   *cause.* It is possible that in addition to its modern meaning the word is here also made to carry the obsolete meaning of 'disease'.

4   *harlot* lewd (used of either sex in Shakespeare's time)

5-6   *blank | And level* (terms from shooting, *blank* being the white spot in the centre of the target, *level* meaning either the action of aiming or the mark aimed at, here probably the latter)

7   *hook to me* get hold of (the metaphor derives from the use of the grappling-hook in sea-fights)

8   *Given to the fire.* Death by fire was the punishment for women found guilty of high treason or of petty treason (the latter consisted in the murder, or connivance at the murder, of husband or master). Leontes believes Hermione to be guilty of both forms of treason (see III.2.13-16).

13   *Conceiving* apprehending the significance of

17   *solely* alone

18   *no thought of him!* let me not think of him (Polixenes)

27   *be second to* support

30   *free* guiltless

35   *heavings* deep groans or sighs

38   *humour* state of mind

39   *presses him from sleep* weighs upon him and prevents him from sleeping

       What noise there, ho? These words suggest that the altercation of lines 26–39 is meant to take place out of the hearing of Leontes.

41   *gossips* godparents (who will be needed at the child's baptism)

47   *dishonesty* dishonourable actions

49   *Commit me for committing honour* send me to prison for doing what is honourable

50   *La you now, you hear.* The words, equivalent to our 'There now, you hear how she will talk', are accompanied by some gesture of resignation.

55-7   *yet that dares | Less appear so in comforting your evils | Than such as most seem yours* yet one who dares to appear less so when it comes to countenancing your crimes than such people as seem most devoted to you

60   *by combat make her good* prove her to be virtuous in a trial by combat (a traditional means of vindicating a lady's honour)

61   *worst* weakest

67   *mankind* mannish, virago-like

68   *intelligencing* acting as go-between

74   *woman-tired* henpecked (from 'tire', a term in falconry, meaning 'to tear a piece of flesh with the beak')

       unroosted driven from your perch

75   *Partlet* (the name of the hen in *Reynard the Fox*, hence a traditional name for a hen)

76   *crone.* The context suggests that the word here does not mean 'withered old woman', which would have little pertinence, but is used in its other sense of 'old ewe'. Paulina's loud reproaches, after being compared to the angry clucking of a hen, are now likened to the bleating of an old ewe.

78   *by that forcèd baseness* under the name of bastard,

which has been thrust upon her (*forcèd* and *put upon* seem to have much the same meaning, being used to reinforce each other)

90   *callat* scold

94-5   *Hence with it, and together with the dam | Commit them to the fire!* This follows *Pandosto*, where Shakespeare read how 'Bellaria was brought to bed of a fair and beautiful daughter, which no sooner Pandosto heard, but he determined that both Bellaria and the young infant should be burnt with fire' (page 192).

96   *th'old proverb*. It is found, for instance, in Overbury's character of a Sergeant: 'The devil calls him his white son; he is so like him that he is the worse for it'.

100   *trick* characteristic form

104   *got* begot

106   *No yellow in't* let there be no yellow (the colour of jealousy) in it

106-7   *lest she suspect, as he does, | Her children not her husband's*. Malone, one of Shakespeare's eighteenth-century editors, thought that 'In the ardour of composition Shakespeare seems here to have forgotten the difference of sexes'. But his fellow-editor, Steevens, was probably right in claiming that 'The seeming absurdity in the last clause of Paulina's ardent address to Nature was undoubtedly designed, being an extravagance characteristically preferable to languid correctness, and chastised declamation'. It is one of the many comic touches in the scene by means of which Shakespeare mitigates its tragic impact upon the audience.

108   *losel* worthless fellow

114-15   *It is an heretic that makes the fire, | Not she which burns in't* if you burn me, it will be you who make the fire who are the heretic, not I who burn in it (the stress of line 114 falls on *makes*). Burning was the extreme punishment for heresy. Paulina wittily applies it to the heresy of lacking faith in Hermione.

126 *A better guiding spirit* someone better fitted than you to guide her

139 *proper* own

147 *beseech'*. The apostrophe, found in F but absent in later Folios, indicates the omission of 'you'.

149 *dear* loving

158 *officious*. The conjunction with *tenderly* suggests that the word has here not its modern meaning but the obsolete one of 'ready to do kind offices'.

159 *Lady Margery*. Since 'margery-prater' was the cant term for a hen, *Lady Margery* may be a variant of *Dame Partlet* (line 75).

161 *this beard's grey*. The reference is not to his own beard, since in the first part of the play Leontes cannot be much more than thirty, but to that of Antigonus, who is described as an old man (by himself in line 165, and by the Shepherd at III.3.103–4). Perhaps Leontes is meant to pull Antigonus's beard, though it would suffice if he pointed at it.

165 *pawn* venture, hazard

167 *Swear by this sword*. It was customary to swear by a sword, since its handle is in the form of a cross.

169 *see'st thou?* do you hear?
fail non-performance

171 *lewd-tongued* foul-mouthed

177 *its*. Here and at III.2.99 F prints *it*, the old form of the possessive pronoun, which was just beginning to be replaced by 'its' when *The Winter's Tale* was written (of the ten instances of 'its' in the entire Folio six come from *The Winter's Tale*).

178 *climate* region, clime

178–82 *As by strange fortune | ... or end it*. The lines paraphrase a passage in *Pandosto*: 'For he found out this device, that seeing, as he thought, it came by fortune, so he would commit it to the charge of fortune' (page 193).

181 *commend it strangely* commit it as a stranger

183

189   *In more than this deed does require* (probably to a greater extent than you deserve by this deed')

191   *loss* perdition, destruction

197   *beyond accompt* (probably 'beyond explanation', rather than 'beyond any of which we have account, unprecedented' or 'beyond calculation', as it is usually glossed)

199   *suddenly* very speedily

201   *session* judicial trial

III.1   Some commentators have located this scene on Delphos. But since the return of Cleomenes and Dion to Sicily is announced in the previous scene, and they call for fresh horses in line 21, its imagined location must be a Sicilian high road, somewhere between the sea-port and the court.

1   *delicate* delightful

4   *habits* vestments

11   *event* outcome

14   *is worth the use* has been well spent

17   *carriage* conduct, management

19   *divine* priest

20   *discover* reveal

III.2   Shakespeare has here fused two court-scenes in *Pandosto* which are separated by several weeks (pages 194–5, 197–8). In each the Queen is accused in open court and defends herself eloquently; some of her words are closely echoed in Hermione's speeches (lines 27–31, 44–6, 113). In *Pandosto* the King immediately accepts the truth of the oracle and repents his actions. By making Leontes blasphemously deny its truth, Shakespeare is able to punctuate his trial-scene with a crescendo of climaxes, culminating in Paulina's report of the Queen's death.

1	*sessions* trial (a collective plural, as again at line 139)
2	*Even pushes 'gainst our heart* strikes even at my heart
7	*purgation* clearing from the suspicion of guilt
10	*Silence!* In F this is printed as *Silence.* towards the right margin, as if it were a stage direction, and some editors have accepted it as such. But most have assigned it as an exclamation to the officer, since it would be a very unusual stage direction but is a traditional law-court cry. The entry of Hermione may be supposed to cause some stir in the court, which must be silenced before the indictment can be read.
17–20	*the pretence whereof being by circumstances partly laid open, thou, Hermione, contrary to the faith and allegiance of a true subject, didst counsel and aid them, for their better safety, to fly away by night.* This follows closely the wording of the indictment in *Pandosto*: 'their pretence being partly spied, she counselled them to fly away by night for their better safety' (page 194).
17	*pretence* purpose, design
27–31	*if powers divine	Behold our human actions – as they do –	I doubt not then but innocence shall make	False accusation blush, and tyranny	Tremble at patience.* This closely follows the Queen's speech in *Pandosto*: 'If the divine powers be privy to human actions – as no doubt they are – I hope my patience shall make fortune blush, and my unspotted life shall stain spiteful discredit' (page 197).
35	*history* story presented on the stage
	pattern match
36	*take* captivate
37	*owe* own
42	*As I weigh grief, which I would spare* as I value grief, which I would do without
43	*a derivative from me to mine* a heritage from me to my children
44	*stand* make a stand, fight
44–6	*I appeal	To your own conscience, sir, before Polixenes	*

    Came to your court, how I was in your grace. Another echo of the Queen's speech in *Pandosto*: 'how I have led my life before Egistus' coming, I appeal, Pandosto, to the gods and to thy conscience' (page 197).

45   *conscience* inward knowledge

48–9   *With what encounter so uncurrent I | Have strained t'appear thus* with what behaviour so out of the ordinary I have transgressed that I should appear thus (in a court of justice). The difficulty of this much debated passage is caused chiefly by a shift in the nature of the appeal: Hermione first begs Leontes to *remember* how, before the arrival of Polixenes, her behaviour merited his love, and next begs him to *make known* how, after the arrival of Polixenes, her behaviour merited his arraignment of her.

54–6   *wanted | Less impudence to gainsay what they did | Than to perform it first.* As often with Shakespeare, an excess of negatives obscures the meaning. The substitution in our minds of 'possessed' for *wanted* makes the sense clear.

58–9   *More than mistress of | Which comes to me in name of fault* to be possessor of more than what may be called a fault (the stress is on *fault*). Hermione acknowledges that she may be guilty of *faults*, but not of the *bolder vices* (line 54) with which she has been charged.

62   *required* deserved

75   *Wotting* if they know

77   *What you have underta'en to do in's absence* (namely to murder Leontes)

80   *level* (the mark shot at)

84   *of your fact* guilty of your deed

85   *concerns more than avails* is of more importance than use to you

86   *like to itself* like the outcast it is

91   *bug* bugbear

92   *commodity* advantage

98   *Starred most unluckily* born under a most unlucky star

100   *post*. Public notices were exhibited on posts in Shakespeare's day.

101   *immodest* immoderate, excessive

103   *of all fashion* of all sorts

104   *i'th'open air*. Fresh air was held to be dangerous for invalids.

105   *strength of limit* strength through resting the prescribed period after childbirth

113   *'Tis rigour and not law*. The phrase comes from *Pandosto*, where the Queen declares that 'if she were condemned without any further proof it was rigour and not law' (page 195).

118   *The Emperor of Russia was my father*. In *Pandosto* it is the wife of Egistus (Shakespeare's Polixenes) who is daughter of the Emperor of Russia.

121   *flatness* absoluteness

131-4   *Hermione is chaste ... be not found*. The words follow for the most part verbatim those of the oracle in *Pandosto* (page 196). In the 1607 edition 'live without an heir' was changed to 'die without an heir', thereby providing our sole piece of evidence that Shakespeare used one of the earlier editions of *Pandosto*.

141   *to report* for reporting

142-3   *conceit and fear | Of the Queen's speed* thinking about and worrying over the Queen's fate

160   *tardied* delayed

161-3   *though I with death and with | Reward did threaten and encourage him, | Not doing it and being done* though I threatened him with death if he did not do it and encouraged him with the promise of reward if he did it

165   *Unclasped my practice* revealed my plot

166   *Which you knew great – and to the hazard*. In the second Folio this line is made regular by the insertion of *certain* before *hazard*. This unnecessary emendation has been adopted by many later editors.

167   *commended* committed

169   *Through*. The word is here pronounced as two syllables.

170   *Woe the while!* (literally 'woe for the present time!')

171   *O cut my lace.* Cleopatra (*Antony and Cleopatra*,
      I.3.71) and Elizabeth (*Richard III*, IV.1.33) make the
      same demand to express their great agitation.
      lace (the lacing of her stays)

175   *In leads or oils* in cauldrons of molten lead or boiling oil

179   *idle* foolish, senseless

182   *spices* slight tastes

184   *That did but show thee of a fool inconstant.* Coleridge's
      paraphrase of this much discussed line, 'show thee,
      being a fool naturally, to have improved thy folly by
      inconstancy', seems to come closest to conveying its
      probable meaning. The nearest parallel to the con-
      struction elsewhere in Shakespeare is found in *3 Henry
      VI*, III.3.24–5: 'That Henry, sole possessor of my love,
      | Is, of a king, become a banished man'.

185–7 *Nor was't much | Thou wouldst have poisoned good
      Camillo's honour | To have him kill a king.* 'How should
      Paulina know this?' asks Malone. 'No one had
      charged the King with this crime except himself,
      while Paulina was absent, attending on Hermione.
      The poet seems to have forgotten this circumstance.'
      Either that or he thought that it would go unnoticed in
      the theatre.

191   *shed water out of fire* shed tears while standing in hell-
      fire

195   *conceive* apprehend that

197– *But the last – O lords, | ... As I would do the gods.*
  205 There is no justification for assuming that Paulina,
      during this speech, is already aware of Hermione's re-
      covery. At this point she is surely meant to be fully
      convinced of her death, so that no deception is in-
      volved in anything she says here.

198   *said* spoken

203   *Tincture or lustre in her lip, her eye* colour in her lip or
      lustre in her eye

210   *still* always

221-2   *Do not receive affliction* | *At my petition* do not give yourself up to affliction because I have urged you to

223   *minded you* put you in mind

228   *remember* remind

229   *Who is lost too.* Since the trial of Hermione follows quickly upon the departure of Antigonus, there is no reason why Paulina should suppose this. But Shakespeare expected his audience not to notice such inconsistencies.

         Take your patience to you arm yourself with patience

238   *recreation* diversion, pastime

239   *exercise.* Both the meaning of 'habitual employment' and that of 'religious observance' would seem to be involved.

240-41   *Come,* | *And lead me to these sorrows.* F's line-division, *Come, and lead me* | *To these sorrows,* which modern editors have taken over with remarkable unanimity, makes the speech peter out in a very un-Shakespearian way. Several redivisions were attempted by eighteenth-century editors. The most satisfactory, which is here adopted, is the one found in Steevens's editions of 1778 and 1785. The long pause after *Come,* which fills out the line, is an expression of the King's anguish.

I.3.1   *perfect* certain

2   *The deserts of Bohemia.* Since the day in 1619 when Ben Jonson, in conversation with William Drummond, ridiculed Shakespeare for endowing Bohemia with a sea-coast, 'where there is no sea near by some 100 miles', a vast deal of ink has been spilt over this howler. Commentators have taken up four main positions: (1) that Shakespeare could never have been guilty of such an error (hence Sir Thomas Hanmer, one of his eighteenth-century editors, throughout his text changed 'Bohemia' to 'Bythinia', claiming that

the former was a printing-house corruption); (2) that no error is involved, since in the late thirteenth and early sixteenth centuries Bohemia actually possessed a bit of sea-coast, or since 'Bohemia' is really another name for 'Apulia', on the south-east coast of Italy; (3) that the error was introduced purposely by Shakespeare in order to convey to his audience that this Bohemia is to be found not on the contemporary map of Europe but in the realms of the imagination – that the sea-coast of Bohemia was perhaps even a standard joke of the time, like Wigan Pier or the Swiss Navy in our day; (4) that Shakespeare simply took over the error from *Pandosto*, being, like most of his contemporaries, rather vague about the geography of Central Europe. This last seems the most plausible explanation. A writer who, in *The Tempest*, can think of Milan as a sea-port, and in *The Two Gentlemen of Verona* can make Valentine sail there from Verona, would not have boggled at a sea-coast for the very much less known Bohemia.

4   *present* imminent
     In my conscience to my mind
10   *loud* rough, stormy
12   *keep* live
15–18 *I have heard, but not believed, the spirits o'th'dead | May walk again : if such thing be, thy mother | Appeared to me last night; for ne'er was dream | So like a waking.* Shakespeare leaves us purposely uncertain whether what Antigonus experienced was a dream or an apparition.
20–21 *I never saw a vessel of like sorrow, | So filled and so becoming.* Although this passage has received a great deal of discussion, this has turned chiefly on the appropriateness of the word *becoming*, which has been often, and quite unnecessarily, emended. The one real problem – whether, with most editors, to place a comma after *sorrow* or whether to follow F, which omits the

comma – has been ignored. Though both readings
make good sense, the one here adopted seems the more
satisfactory. The reference is to the intensity of
Hermione's sorrow, coupled with the grace with which
she bears it. The same metaphor is found in *Julius
Caesar* (V.5.13–14): 'Now is that noble vessel full of
grief, | That it runs over even at his eyes.'

32   *Perdita*. This name, meaning 'the lost one', follows the
precedent of Marina, named thus 'For she was born at
sea' (*Pericles*, III.3.13).

35   *shrieks* (the typical cry of a ghost)

38   *toys* things of no value or substance

39   *superstitiously*. The primary meaning seems to be
'punctiliously', but the modern meaning may be also
present, producing a kind of pun.

40   *squared* ruled, regulated

46   *thy character* the written account of you (*the letters of
Antigonus* referred to at V.2.33–4)
(stage direction) *he lays down a box*. Most editors
follow Dr Johnson in making Antigonus lay down 'a
bundle', misled, it seems, by the *fardel* referred to
repeatedly in IV.4.703 ff. But the Shepherd there
speaks of *this fardel and box* (IV.4.752–3). The box is
clearly the one in which the gold was stored, while the
fardel consists of the bearing-cloth (III.3.111) and the
mantle (V.2.32) in which the child was wrapped, if
these are not, in fact, one and the same garment.
these (the pieces of gold in the box)

47   *both breed thee, pretty, | And still rest thine* be enough to
pay for your upbringing, pretty one, and still remain
yours (because most of it will be unspent)

50   *loss* the condition of being lost
Weep I cannot. The words presumably glance back at
There weep, and leave it crying (line 31).

53–4   *Thou'rt like to have | A lullaby too rough*. This echoes
the Queen's words in *Pandosto*: 'Shalt thou have the
whistling winds for thy lullaby . . .?' (page 193).

55–6   *A savage clamour! | Well may I get aboard! This is the chase.* 'This clamour was the cry of the dogs and hunters; then seeing the bear, he cries, "This is the chase", or, *the animal pursued*', explained Dr Johnson, and most commentators have agreed with him. The Shepherd's reference to a hunt in the lines that follow seems to support this explanation. Yet it is unacceptable for several reasons: (1) if the hunters are in such close pursuit of the bear that their voices can be heard off stage, it does not make sense that they let him devour Antigonus at his leisure, and are never heard of again; (2) the epithet *savage* is far more suited to the growling of the bear than to the cry of the dogs and hunters. The word *clamour* was used of any 'loud vocal noise of beasts and birds' (*Oxford English Dictionary*); (3) *Well may I get aboard!* suggests a threat to Antigonus's life, which fits the bear but not the hunt. *The chase* then means not 'the hunted animal' (a possible meaning of *chase*) but rather 'the hunt'.

57   (stage direction) *Exit, pursued by a bear.* The question whether Shakespeare's company here used a real bear or an actor dressed in a bear's skin has been much debated. There is a good deal of evidence of various kinds that bears in Elizabethan and Jacobean plays and masques were impersonated by actors dressed in bearskins, none that a real bear was ever used. Even if it had been possible to train such an animal to run across the stage at the required moment – and this seems most unlikely – Shakespeare's evident desire to rob the death of Antigonus of its horror by adding touches of comedy would have made him prefer the use of an actor in a bear's skin (see Introduction, page 17).

61   *ancientry* old folk. He is thinking of himself. In contrast to the shepherd in *Pandosto*, he is depicted as an old man, already sixty-seven when he finds the child (since at IV.4.450 he speaks of himself as *a man of*

fourscore three). For reasons suggested in the Introduction (pages 20–21), he had to be an old man for Shakespeare's purposes. But the change of age makes his supposed paternity of Perdita much less credible.

62 *Hark you now*. A number of editors take these words to refer to the sound of the hunt off stage and introduce the stage direction *Horns*. More probably they are addressed to the audience, drawing their attention to what the Shepherd is going to tell them.

62–3 *boiled brains* (probably 'addle-brained youths', rather than 'hotheads' or 'lunatics', as it is usually explained)

66–7 *by the seaside, browsing of ivy*. This is an echo of *Pandosto*'s 'to see if perchance the sheep was browsing on the sea ivy, whereon they greatly do feed' (page 199).

67 *Good luck, an't be thy will!* send me good luck, if it be thy (God's) will! The reference is to the search for the sheep, not to the finding of the child, as many editors, misled by F's punctuation, *Good-lucke (and't be thy will) what haue we heere?*, think.

68 *barne* child (a dialect form, but not confined to the North in Shakespeare's day)

69 *child* a female infant (a dialect form found predominantly in the West country)

70 *scape* escapade, slip (especially of a sexual nature)

72–3 *some stair-work, some trunk-work, some behind-door-work*. The reference seems to be not, as has been claimed, to the way in which the lover got access to his mistress – by back stairs, by concealment in a trunk, by hiding behind doors – but rather to the places where the furtive copulation took place. 'Work' is used repeatedly by Shakespeare in the sense of 'sexual intercourse'.

75 *hallowed* shouted

81–102 *I have seen two such sights ... he's at it now*. The Clown's account of the deaths of Antigonus and the mariners is purposely made to sound ridiculous in order to 'distance' them from the audience and so to reduce their horror and pathos. This device of turning horror into comedy is by no means unique with Shakespeare. It is only the way he does it here that is unique. It is done chiefly (1) by making the Clown, anxious to narrate both calamities at the same time, scuttle to and fro between them; (2) by means of the figurative language he employs. The comic effect is achieved by the opposite means from that used in the mock-heroic: there it results from the discrepancy between the trivial events and the grandiose manner in which these are described; here it results from the discrepancy between extraordinary and fearful events and the homely and trivial manner in which these are described.

87   *takes up.* The primary meaning is probably 'swallows up', with the meaning 'rebukes' perhaps also present as a quibble.

91   *yeast* foam (compare *Macbeth*, IV.1.52–3, 'though the yesty waves | Confound and swallow navigation up')

92   *land-service* military, as opposed to naval, service (hence Antigonus as opposed to the sailors). The choice of the word was, perhaps, determined by another sense of 'service', 'that which is served up for a meal', and this meaning may be present as a quibble.

95   *flap-dragoned it* swallowed it up as one would a flap-dragon (a small object, usually a raisin, which floated in a glass of lighted spirits and had to be swallowed)

106–7 *there your charity would have lacked footing.* This is probably a quibble on two meanings of *footing*: (1) foothold; (2) establishment (of a charitable foundation).

111   *bearing-cloth* (the wrap in which a child was carried to church for baptism)

114–15 *changeling.* Since it was believed that fairies steal beautiful children, leaving their own ugly and misshapen ones in the cradle, *changeling* must here refer to the human child, stolen by the fairies because of its beauty.

116   *made*. F prints *mad*, but the emendation, first made in the eighteenth century by Theobald, is undoubtedly right, and is supported by *Pandosto*, where the shepherd tells his wife that 'if she could hold her peace they were made for ever' (page 201).

117   *well to live* well-to-do, prosperous

120   *close* secret (since to make known the possession of fairies' gifts was held to bring misfortune)

        next nearest

121   *still* for ever

126   *curst* savage

131   *Marry* indeed

IV.1   (stage direction) *Enter Time, the Chorus*. Time is here depicted as he traditionally appears in pictures: an old man with wings (line 4), bearing an hour-glass (line 16). Another of his conventional attributes, the scythe, is not mentioned, and may have been omitted on the stage in order to emphasize his role in the play as revealer rather than as destroyer. The use of Time as chorus bridging the gap between the two parts of the play is analogous to that of Rumour at the opening of *2 Henry IV*, and was presumably suggested by the title-page of Greene's novel, which reads: 'Pandosto. The Triumph of Time. Wherein is discovered by a pleasant History that although by the means of sinister fortune Truth may be concealed, yet by Time, in spite of fortune, it is most manifestly revealed.... *Temporis filia veritas* ...'. Many critics have assigned Time's speech to a collaborator, refusing to believe that Shakespeare could have written such lame and bald verse. But it would seem to be purposely lame, bald, and garrulous in order to characterize the speaker; and the need for an idiom strongly marked off from the dramatic verse of the play helps to account for the absence of the unmistakable voice of Shakespeare (its closest parallel in style and matter is the Chorus-speech of Gower in *Pericles*, IV.4).

1   *try* test

1-2   *both joy and terror | Of good and bad.* Probably not, as it is commonly explained, 'the joy of the good and the terror of the bad', but rather 'the joy as well as the terror of good and bad alike'. This accords much better not only with the facts of life but also with the words that follow: by making error, Time is the joy of the bad and the terror of the good; by unfolding it, the terror of the bad and the joy of the good (compare *The Rape of Lucrece*, line 995, 'O time, thou tutor both to good and bad').

3   *in the name of* under the designation of (he is telling the slow-witted members of the audience who he is)

6-7   *and leave the growth untried | Of that wide gap* and leave unexamined what has happened during that long interval

7-9   *since it is in my power | To o'erthrow law, and in one self-born hour | To plant and o'erwhelm custom.* The *law* referred to is evidently that established by Renaissance critics, who, insisting on 'unity of time', limited the action of a play to one day (in *Hamlet*, II.2.396, Polonius speaks of 'the law of writ and the liberty', meaning plays adhering to the rules of writing laid down by academic critics and plays which ignored all such rules). Shakespeare wittily makes Time defend his own most blatant violation of the rule of unity of time in this play by having him point out that all such laws and customs are of no permanent validity. The crime referred to in lines 4-7 is therefore that of violating the rule of the unity of time, rather than – as the wording suggests – that of failing to stage the events of the intervening sixteen years.

8   *one self-born hour* (probably 'one hour to which I my-

self have given birth': all hours were thought of as the
offspring of time)

9–11   *Let me pass | The same I am ere ancient'st order was | Or
what is now received.* This obscure sentence seems to
carry on the thought of the preceding lines: 'Allow me
to pass, who am the same that I was before the oldest
injunctions became established or what is now accepted as authoritative'. The use of *I am* for 'I was',
though odd, can be defended as appropriate to Time,
who sees himself as standing outside the flow of events.
The use of *witness* for 'witnessed' in line 11 may be a
parallel case, though here one is tempted to emend,
since F's *witnesse* could easily be a misreading of *wit-
nessd* in the manuscript.

10   *order* injunction

11   *received* accepted as a rule

16   *I turn my glass.* Time here turns the hour-glass which
he carries in his hands, thus marking the commence-
ment of the second half of the play.
scene play presented on the stage

17   *As* as if

17–18 *Leontes leaving – | Th'effects of his fond jealousies so
grieving* leaving Leontes – who is filled with such grief
by the effects of his foolish jealousies

22   *I mentioned.* As in line 16 (*my scene*), Time and the
playwright are here identified. The attractive suggestion has been made that this may be due to the circumstance that, in the first performances of the play,
Shakespeare himself took the part of Time, and that
the references to *my scene* and *I mentioned* were inserted as jests for those members of the audience who
recognized this fact.
Florizel. The name seems to have been derived from
Amadis de Grecia, a Spanish continuation of *Amadis de
Gaule*. In it a Prince Florisel disguises himself as a
shepherd in order to woo a beautiful shepherdess, who,
unknown to herself, is really a princess.

25   *Equal with wond'ring* (probably 'just as much as men's wonder at it has grown')

26   *list not* do not care to

28   *what to her adheres* what belongs to her story
      after. The 'f' was probably silent, so that the word rhymed with *daughter.*

29   *argument* theme

31   *yet that Time himself doth say* yet allow that Time himself says

IV.2.4   *fifteen.* This is presumably a slip, since Time (IV.1.6), Paulina (V.3.31), and Camillo elsewhere (V.3.50) all speak of sixteen years, following *Pandosto* in this.

5   *been aired abroad* lived abroad

7   *feeling* heartfelt

8   *allay* means of abatement
     I o'erween I am presumptuous enough

13   *want* lack

17   *considered* requited

19   *the heaping friendships* the heaping up of your friendly services

27   *approved* proved

31   *missingly* regretfully

32   *frequent to* addicted to

35-6   *eyes under my service which look upon his removedness* servants in my employ, who are spying on him during his absences from court

45   *angle* fish-hook

47   *question* talk

IV.3.1   *peer* (probably 'appear' (as in IV.4.3) rather than 'peep out')

2   *doxy* beggar's wench

3   *sweet* pleasant part

4   *pale* domain, bounds. The choice of the word was no

doubt determined by the preceding *red*. Since *pale* also
meant 'pallor', both the meaning of 'The red blood
reigns in the former domain of winter' and that of
'The red blood reigns in place of the pallor of winter'
may be intended to be present.

7   *Doth set my pugging tooth an edge.* Since 'to pug'
means 'to pull, tug', the *pugging tooth* presumably
refers to a taste for stealing sheets by pulling them off
the hedges (*tooth* meaning 'taste', 'liking'). Most
editors emend F's *an edge* to *on edge*, but this produces
the opposite sense from the one required: that of a
revulsion against 'pugging' rather than of a whetting
of the appetite for it, which 'to set an edge' must mean
here.

8   *For a quart of ale is a dish for a king.* The ale is to be
bought with the money received for the stolen sheets.

10   *With heigh, with heigh, the thrush and the jay.* F reads
With heigh, the Thrush and the Iay. The duplication of
With heigh, first found in the second Folio, has been
adopted by most subsequent editors. Yet the pattern of
the other two stanzas suggests that something else has
dropped out, perhaps the name of another bird.

11   *aunts* (a cant term for loose women)

14   *three-pile* (the most costly kind of velvet)

15-18 *But shall I go mourn for that, my dear? | The pale moon
shines by night : | And when I wander here and there | I
then do most go right* but shall I mourn because I am
out of service? On moonlight nights, when I am
wandering about (looking for things to steal), I am
living the life which is right for me

19-22 *If tinkers may have leave to live, | And bear the sow-skin
budget, | Then my account I well may give, | And in the
stocks avouch it* so long as tinkers are allowed to prac-
tise their trade, and carry their pigskin tool-bag, I
shall be well able to account for myself, and, if they put
me in the stocks, affirm it (that I am a tinker and no
vagabond). Vagabonds and beggars were commonly

set in the stocks in Shakespeare's day. Autolycus
carries a leather bag (*budget*) with a tinker's tools to
escape arrest as a vagabond. It was not uncommon for
thieves to pose as tinkers.

23-4   *My traffic is sheets; when the kite builds, look to lesser
linen.* The kite was notorious for stealing small pieces of
linen for nest-building. Autolycus specializes in the
stealing of sheets, which he then sells.

23   *traffic* saleable commodities, merchandise

24   *Autolycus.* The name is derived from Greek myth, in
which Autolycus is the son of Hermes and the grand-
father of Odysseus. He is referred to in the *Odyssey* as
one 'who excelled all men in thievery and in oaths',
and in Ovid's *Metamorphoses* as 'a wily pie, | And such
a fellow as in theft and filching had no peer' (Book XI,
Golding's translation).

         who. This refers back to *My father*, not to *Autolycus*.

25   *littered under Mercury* born when the planet Mercury
was in the ascendant. The god Mercury was the patron
of thieves. As the conception of the planets had become
fused with that of the gods after whom they were
named, the influence of the planet Mercury was believed to promote thievery. Autolycus therefore jestingly attributes his and his father's propensity for
stealing to Mercury's ascendancy at their birth.

26-7   *With die and drab I purchased this caparison* gaming and
whoring brought me to these rags (literally 'Through
dice and harlot I procured this apparel')

27   *my revenue is the silly cheat* (either 'My income consists in humble booty' or 'My income derives from
simple trickery'; Autolycus is contrasting his lowly but
comparatively safe way of making a living with the
risky life of the highwayman)

27-8   *Gallows and knock* hanging (the punishment for high-
way robbery) and hard blows (which the highwayman
may receive from his intended victim)

29   *For the life to come* (probably 'as for the life in the next

world', rather than simply 'as for the future'; like Macbeth, who is ready to 'jump the life to come' if he can escape punishment in this world (*Macbeth*, I.7.7), Autolycus refuses to worry about divine punishment in the after-life)

31 *every 'leven wether tods* every eleven sheep yield a tod (28 lb.) of wool

34 *cock* woodcock (a proverbially foolish bird)

39–40 *made me* (the ethical dative) made

40–41 *three-man-song men* (singers of secular part-songs for male voices: treble, tenor, and bass)

41–3 *but they are most of them means and basses – but one Puritan amongst them, and he sings psalms to hornpipes.* F, followed by most editors, places a semicolon after *basses*, thus making the Clown remark that there is only one Puritan among them, as if Puritan and treble voice were synonymous, which they were not. Sense is restored by changing the semicolon to a dash, which makes the Clown add: 'except for one Puritan amongst them (who takes the treble part), and he sings psalms even to lively dance-tunes'. The emphasis seems to be on *psalms*, asserting the devoutness of the Puritan, rather than on *hornpipes*, which would assert his cheerfulness.

44 *warden pies* pies made with warden pears (a kind of cooking pear)

45 *out of my note* not on my list

47 *o'th'sun* sun-dried (as distinct from oven-dried)

50 *I'th'name of me!* Though no other instance of this exclamation has been discovered, there is a close parallel in Sir Andrew's 'Before me' (*Twelfth Night*, II.3.171). The Act of Abuses (1606), which forbade the vain use of the name of God in stage plays, may be accountable for the unusual, and no doubt intentionally comic, form of the exclamation.

55 *offend.* In the second Folio and most subsequent editions this is changed to *offends.* But it is merely one of

the several instances in the play of the 'plural by attraction' (as, for example, at IV.2.24 and 30).

63   *a horseman or a footman* a mounted highwayman or a footpad

85   *troll-my-dames*. Troll-my-dame is a game, also called 'troll-madam' (from the French *trou-madame*), which is played by 'trolling' balls through hoops set on a board. Since 'to troll' also meant 'to stroll', as well as 'to circulate, be passed round', it seems likely that Autolycus is quibbling on the name of the game, alluding in fact to loose women, his *aunts*.

90   *no more but abide* (probably 'make only a brief stay', since an obsolete meaning of *abide* is 'to wait before proceeding further, to pause'; the *Oxford English Dictionary*, however, records no occurrences of this meaning later than the early sixteenth century)

92   *ape-bearer* showman who travels about with a performing monkey

       process-server sheriff's officer who serves summonses (much the same as *bailiff*)

93–4   *compassed a motion of the Prodigal Son* acquired a puppet-show representing the story of the Prodigal Son (puppet-shows depicting scenes from the Bible were common in Shakespeare's day)

95   *living* property, estate

98   *Prig* thief

105   *I am false of heart that way* my heart fails me in such matters

110   *softly* slowly

116   *Your purse is not hot enough to purchase your spice*. Since 'a cold purse' meant 'an empty purse', Autolycus is able to quibble on the nature of spices and the state of the Clown's purse.

118   *cheat* rogue's trick

119   *unrolled* struck off the roll (of the fraternity of rogues)

122   *hent* take hold of (in order to leap over)

IV.4   In *Pandosto* there is no sheep-shearing feast, only 'a meeting of all the farmers' daughters in Sicilia, whither Fawnia was also bidden as the mistress of the feast' (page 204). It is on her return from this feast that she and the Prince first set eyes on each other.

1   *weeds* garments

2–3   *no shepherdess, but Flora | Peering in April's front*. The words were suggested by a passage in *Pandosto*, telling how Fawnia kept her sheep, 'defending her face from the heat of the sun with no other veil but with a garland made of boughs and flowers, which attire became her so gallantly as she seemed to be the goddess Flora herself for beauty' (page 202). At the feast Perdita is presumably garlanded and bedecked with flowers, while Florizel, following the example of the Prince in *Pandosto*, is dressed as a shepherd swain.

3   *Peering in April's front* appearing at the beginning of April (compare IV.3.1)

4   *petty* minor

6   *extremes* extravagances

8   *mark o'th'land* object of everyone's attention

9   *wearing* garments

10   *But that* were it not that

11   *mess*. The sequence of metaphors makes it probable that the meaning here is 'dish' or 'course of dishes', rather than 'a group of persons who were served together at table', which is its meaning at I.2.227.

12   *with accustom*. Editors have retained F's *with a Custome*, explaining it as meaning 'from habit'. But as no parallels to this phrase are to be found, Dover Wilson's suggested emendation 'with accustom' has been adopted. 'Accustom', an obsolete word meaning 'habit' or 'habituation', was still in use in the seventeenth century. The fact of a misreading is all the more probable as two further errors of transcription occur within the same two lines in a text which is remarkably free from such errors.

13   *swoon.* This emendation of F's *sworne*, first suggested in the eighteenth century by Theobald, and adopted by the majority of subsequent editors, almost certainly restores the right reading. Those who retain *sworn* usually explain the passage as meaning that Florizel, in putting on a *swain's wearing*, would seem to have sworn to show Perdita as in a mirror what she herself really is (or, alternatively, how she ought to be attired).

14–16   *I bless the time | When my good falcon made her flight across | Thy father's ground.* This was suggested by *Pandosto*, where the first encounter of the lovers is described as taking place when the Prince was hawking.

17   *difference* (of rank)

21–2   *his work, so noble, | Vilely bound up.* The reverse of this metaphor from book-binding is found in Juliet's 'Was ever book containing such vile matter | So fairly bound?' (*Romeo and Juliet*, III.2.83–4). There the binding stands for Romeo's whole exterior, here it stands only for Florizel's garments.

22   *Vilely* meanly, wretchedly

23   *flaunts* ostentatious finery

25–31   *The gods themselves, | . . . As I seem now.* The passage is based on some lines in *Pandosto* in which the Prince soliloquizes: 'And yet, Dorastus, shame not at thy shepherd's weed. The heavenly gods have sometime earthly thoughts. Neptune became a ram, Jupiter a bull, Apollo a shepherd . . .' (page 210). No lines illustrate better Shakespeare's power of transmuting the lead he borrows into gold.

32   *piece* person. The word was free from any derogatory sense, and is often used by Shakespeare in the Last Plays to designate a woman.

33   *in a way so chaste* undertaken with so chaste a purpose

35   *faith* pledge, promise (to marry her)

38–40   *One of these two must be necessities, | Which then will speak: that you must change this purpose | Or I my life.* Some commentators take *Or I my life* to mean 'or I

change my life' (from joy to grief). But the two necessities are alternatives, and the sentence apparently
contains a zeugma: 'Either you will have to give up
your resolution to marry me or, should you adhere to
it, I shall lose my life.' That Perdita's fear of forfeiting
her life is not fanciful is shown by the threats of
Polixenes later in the scene.

41   *forced* strained, unnatural

42–3   *Or ... | Or* either ... or

46   *gentle* (an appellation somewhat like 'dearest')

54   (stage direction) *Mopsa, Dorcas*. Mopsa is the name of
the shepherd's wife in *Pandosto*, here given to a young
shepherdess; Dorcas is a woman's name in the Bible
(Acts 9.36).

56   *pantler* servant in charge of the pantry
       butler servant in charge of the cellar

57   *dame* mistress (of a household)

60   *On his shoulder* at his shoulder

60–62   *her face o'fire | With labour, and the thing she took to
quench it : | She would to each one sip.* Many recent
editors have followed F's punctuation, *her face o'fire |
With labour, and the thing she took to quench it | She
would to each one sip.* This is, no doubt, a possible
reading. But the one resulting from the punctuation
here adopted sounds less awkward and more Shakespearian: *the thing she took to quench* the fire had the
effect of inflaming it all the more, just as the wind of
the fans, which was meant to cool Cleopatra's face,
'did seem | To glow the delicate cheeks which they did
cool, | And what they undid did' (*Antony and Cleo-
patra*, II.2.207–9).

66   *more known* better acquainted

75   *Seeming and savour* appearance and scent

76   *Grace and remembrance*. In the flower-symbolism of
Shakespeare's day rosemary stood for remembrance,
while rue, which was also called 'herb of grace', stood
for sorrow or repentance. Perdita wishes her guests

divine favour and to be remembered after their death.

79–82 *Sir, the year growing ancient, | Not yet on summer's death nor on the birth | Of trembling winter, the fairest flowers o'th'season | Are our carnations and streaked gillyvors.* Some commentators have taken these lines to indicate that the sheep-shearing feast takes place in the autumn. But Perdita is not saying that it is *now* autumn, but that in autumn the fairest flowers of that season are carnations etc. Sheep-shearings in Shakespeare's day normally took place late in June, and that is, no doubt, the time-setting he imagined for this scene.

82 *gillyvors* gillyflowers, clove-scented pinks

83 *bastards* hybrids (the streaks being produced by the crossing of different varieties of the plant)

86–103 *For I have heard it said . . . | Desire to breed by me.* The matter of this debate was familiar to many in Shakespeare's audience. He makes Perdita uphold the primitivist point of view, most notably expressed by Montaigne in his essay 'Of the Cannibals', where he asserts the superiority of so-called 'savages' to civilized men and, by analogy, of wild to cultivated fruits. In lines which shortly precede the passage that Shakespeare drew on (in Florio's translation) for the description of Gonzalo's ideal commonwealth in *The Tempest* (II.1.150 ff.), Montaigne uses the word 'bastardized' of cultivated fruits, and declares that 'there is no reason art should gain the point of honour of our great and puissant mother Nature' (Florio's Montaigne, 1603 edition). The argument put forward by Polixenes – that the art by means of which man improves the products of Nature is itself the creation of Nature – was equally familiar.

89 *mean* agency, means

90 *But* unless

90–92 *so over that art | Which you say adds to Nature is an art |*

That Nature makes. Polixenes seems to be saying that Nature's creation of the means of her own improvement (through grafting or crossing) is itself an art which is above that of the gardener, since his art is dependent upon it. The emendation of *over* to 'even', though not essential, is tempting, as it gives the speech much greater clarity.

97   *So it is.* It is possible that Perdita is here momentarily thinking of herself in relation to Florizel. But it may be merely polite assent without real conviction. The dramatic irony of the whole debate is heightened if both disputants are oblivious throughout of its apparent relevance to the intended marriage of the young lovers. Behind it lies the further irony that, unknown to them all, the debate possesses in fact no true relevance to their situation, since Perdita is actually as gentle a scion as is Florizel.

101–3   *No more than, were I painted, I would wish | This youth should say 'twere well, and only therefore | Desire to breed by me.* Perdita's analogy is altogether apposite: in the use of cosmetics as in the crossing of plants Nature's handiwork is being sophisticated by man's efforts to improve it. Perdita's distaste for this is all of a piece with her revulsion against being *Most goddesslike pranked up* (line 10).

103–8   *Here's flowers for you: | . . . Y'are very welcome.* Some commentators believe these lines to be addressed to another group of guests. It seems much more probable that Perdita is trying to make amends for her previous indiscretion (in giving Polixenes and Camillo flowers of winter) by now giving them flowers of summer, thus suggesting that she considers them to be 'men of middle age'.

104   *Hot lavender.* Herbs were divided into 'hot' and 'cold' according to their supposed temperatures, lavender being classed among the 'hot'.

105–6   *The marigold, that goes to bed with' sun | And with him rises weeping.* The reference is to the heliotropic nature of the flower, which closes its petals when the sun sets and opens them again, wet with dew, when it rises.

105   *with' sun.* The apostrophe, found in F, indicates the omission of the definite article.

116–18   *O Proserpina, | For the flowers now that, frighted, thou let'st fall | From Dis's wagon!* Shakespeare is here evidently recalling Ovid's account of the rape of Proserpina (*Metamorphoses*, V.398 ff.), probably in Golding's translation (1567).

118   *Dis's wagon* Pluto's chariot

119   *take* bewitch, enchant

121–2   *sweeter than the lids of Juno's eyes | Or Cytherea's breath* sweeter to *behold* than the lids of Juno's eyes, sweeter to *smell* than the breath of Venus

122   *Cytherea.* The stress falls on the third syllable. Venus was called Cytherea after Cythera, the island where she first stepped ashore after her birth in the seafoam.

122–4   *pale primroses, | That die unmarried ere they can behold | Bright Phoebus in his strength.* In contrast with the marigold, which is also called *Sponsus Solis*, the spouse of the sun, the primrose is pictured as dying unmarried, in early spring, before the bridegroom, Phoebus (the sun), has reached manhood.

124–5   *a malady | Most incident to maids.* The difficulty of this phrase springs from the omission of one important link in the chain of analogy between primroses and young girls: the *malady | Most incident to maids*, from which the primrose is imagined as dying, is the green-sickness. The pale or yellowy-green complexion of girls suffering from this ailment corresponds to the colour of the primrose. The analogy is strengthened by the legend, current in Shakespeare's day, that unmarried young girls who died from this malady were turned into primroses.

126   *crown imperial* the tall, yellow fritillary (which had been

introduced into England from Constantinople in the
1590s)

127   *flower-de-luce* (probably the iris, which was not un-
commonly classed among the lilies)

129   *What, like a corse?* It was customary to strew flowers
upon the bodies of the dead.

130   *Love.* The reference seems to be to Cupid, the god of
love, and F's capital 'L' has therefore been retained.

132   *quick* alive (the word *corse* in Elizabethan usage could
mean a living as well as a dead body)

134   *Whitsun pastorals.* A variety of theatrical entertainments, including Robin Hood plays, were performed
at Whitsuntide in Shakespeare's day.

135–6   *What you do* | *Still betters what is done* whatever you
do seems always better than what you have done
before

143–6   *Each your doing,* | *So singular in each particular,* |
Crowns what you are doing in the present deeds, | *That
all your acts are queens* everything you do, so peerless
in every point, makes whatever you are doing at the
moment seem supreme, so that all your acts are queens

146   *Doricles* (the name which Florizel has assumed in his
disguise as a shepherd)

147   *large* lavish

148   *blood* (probably pronounced here as two syllables)

152   *skill* cause

154–5   *so turtles pair,* | *That never mean to part.* Turtle doves
were believed to remain true to their mates for life.
F omits the comma after *pair*, and is followed in this
by later editors. But the statement is non-restrictive.
Florizel is speaking not of 'those turtles that never
mean to part' but of *all* turtles.

155   *I'll swear for 'em* I'll be sworn they do

162–7   *Come on, strike up!* ... *Come, strike up!* The accident
that several of these lines can be read as blank verse has
led most editors since the eighteenth century to set the
passage out as such, in spite of the fact that in F it is

set out as prose and that the Clown, Mopsa, and Dorcas speak nowhere else in verse.

163–4   *garlic to mend her kissing with!* let her take garlic to overcome her bad breath

165   *in good time!* (here an expression of indignation)

166   *stand upon* value, set store by

170   *and boasts himself.* Probably 'and, they say, he boasts himself ...' is to be understood, setting off what others say about Doricles from what he himself has told the old Shepherd.

171   *a worthy feeding* a valuable grazing-ground

178   *another* the other
      featly nimbly

183–4   *at the door.* This and the reference in lines 338–9 show that Shakespeare imagined an indoor setting for the scene.

186   *several* a good many
      tell count

187   *as* as though
      ballads. The reference throughout is to the popular broadsheet ballad, written in doggerel verse on some sensational topic of the day, and sung to a familiar tune.

191   *pleasant* merry, funny

192   *lamentably* mournfully

193   *sizes* kinds

194   *milliner* vendor of such articles of apparel as gloves and ribbons, haberdasher

196–7   *with such delicate burdens of dildos and fadings, jump her and thump her.* The joke here is that the Servant, while claiming Autolycus's songs to be free from bawdry, unwittingly reveals them to be full of it. The word *dildo* occurs in the refrains of many ballads of the period, but often, through its meaning of 'phallus', with a bawdy connotation. *Fading* was the name of a dance, and the refrain 'With a fading, fading, fading' is found in a ribald popular song of Shakespeare's time.

196   *delicate burdens* delightful refrains

197–200 *and where some stretch-mouthed rascal would, as it were,*
mean mischief, and break a foul gap into the matter, he
makes the maid to answer, 'Whoop, do me no harm, good
man'. The probable meaning of this much debated and
often emended passage is that where the wooer in the
song would interrupt its progress (*break a foul gap into*
the matter) by means of some bawdy action, the girl
checks him with her answer.

198 *stretch-mouthed* wide-mouthed

200 *'Whoop, do me no harm, good man'* (the refrain of a
ribald ditty of the time)

204 *admirable* to be wondered at
conceited witty, ingenious

205 *unbraided* (probably 'not soiled or faded')

207 *points* tagged laces for attaching the hose to the
doublet, lacing a bodice, etc. (with a quibble on 'legal
points')

208 *by th'gross* in large quantities

209 *inkles* linen tapes
caddisses (short for 'caddis ribbons') worsted tapes
used for garters

211 *sleevehand* wristband

212 *square* square piece of material covering the breast

217 *You have of these pedlars* there are pedlars

219 *go about to* wish to

221 *Cypress* (a crape-like fabric)

222 *Gloves as sweet as damask roses.* Gloves were often perfumed.

223 *Masks for faces, and for noses.* Masks to protect the
whole face or the nose only against the sun were commonly worn by ladies in Shakespeare's day.

224 *Bugle-bracelet* bracelet of tube-shaped glass beads,
usually black

228 *poking-sticks* rods used for stiffening the plaits of ruffs

229–30 *What maids lack from head to heel | Come buy of me.*
The colon which is found in F after *heel* and which
subsequent editors have retained (or replaced by a full

stop or exclamation mark) seems intrusive and has therefore been omitted.

234   *bondage* condition of being tied up (into a parcel)

235   *against* in time for

240   *paid you more* (got you with child)

242-3 *Will they wear their plackets where they should bear their faces?* The word *placket* was used for petticoats or the slit in petticoats, and hence also for the pudendum. This last is almost certainly its meaning in line 606, and possibly here, though it seems more probable that the Clown is saying by means of a clothes-metaphor (*placket* = petticoat): 'will they display openly what they should keep hidden?'

245   *kiln-hole* fire-hole of a kiln (a favourite place for gossiping)

      to whistle of to speak secretly of. Since Shakespeare nowhere else uses the word in this sense, the emendation 'to whistle off', adopted by many editors, may be justified ('to whistle off' is a term in falconry, meaning 'to release').

247   *Clamor your tongues.* There has been a great deal of discussion of the meaning of *Clamor*, ever since, in the eighteenth century, Warburton suggested that it was a technical term from bell-ringing: to 'clamor' or 'clammer' meant to increase the strokes of the clapper preparatory to stopping altogether. There is some evidence that this gave rise to the further meaning 'to proceed from noise to silence'. The Clown would then be saying 'Put an end to the tolling of your tongues'. The choice of metaphor seems certainly very suited to the Clown, unlike the emendation 'Charm your tongues', which many editors have preferred.

248-9 *tawdry-lace* silk necktie (much worn by women in Shakespeare's day; so called from Saint Audrey)

249   *sweet* perfumed

256   *parcels of charge* items of value

258   *a-life* dearly

260–79 *Here's one to a very doleful tune ... and as true.*
Shakespeare here provides an extravagant parody of
some of the topics of the ballads of his time, which
dealt in marvels that were claimed to be strictly true,
and were sometimes attested by witnesses.

262 *at a burden* at one birth. The word was used by
Shakespeare in this rare sense only once before, in *The
Comedy of Errors*, V.1.342: 'That bore thee at a burden
two fair sons'.

263 *carbonadoed* scored across and broiled upon the coals

266 *Bless* guard, keep

281 *hands* signatures

286 *passing* exceedingly

288 *westward* in the West country (a pointer that the
scene's location in Shakespeare's mind is England
rather than Bohemia)

294 *Have at it* I will attempt it

295– *Get you hence, for I must go.* | *... Say, whither?* The
306 words of this song are clearly those of 'Two maids
wooing a man', not those of Autolycus's *merry ballad*,
which are to be sung to the same tune. When Mopsa
says *We can both sing it. If thou'lt bear a part, thou shalt
hear* (lines 290–91) she evidently means not only the
tune but also the words of 'Two maids wooing a man'.
There is therefore no indication that she and Dorcas
can read either words or music, as has been claimed
for them. Like Autolycus, they sing the song from
memory.

295–6 *go.* | *Where.* F and most subsequent editors omit the
stop after *go*, but the wording seems to require its insertion.

301 *Or ... or* either ... or

308 *sad* serious

317 *toys* trifling ornaments

320–21 *Money's a meddler* | *That doth utter all men's ware-a*
money has a share in everything, putting all men's ware
in circulation

323–4   *that have made themselves all men of hair* (by dressing themselves in skins in order to look like satyrs; dances of satyrs were not uncommon in medieval and Renaissance entertainments)

325   *Saltiers* (the Servant's blunder for *satyrs*)

326   *gallimaufry* ridiculous medley

328   *bowling* (regarded by the Servant as a gentle, quiet game)

334–5   *One three of them, by their own report, sir, hath danced before the King.* It seems probable that we have here a topical allusion to the performance of Ben Jonson's *The Masque of Oberon* before King James and his court on 1 January 1611. This contained an anti-masque dance of ten or twelve satyrs, described by Jonson as 'an antic dance, full of gesture, and swift motion'. Since the anti-masque dances in court-masques were performed by professional actors, it is quite possible that some, if not all, of the actors who performed the satyrs' dance in *The Winter's Tale* had also performed it in *The Masque of Oberon*, and that the Servant's reference was meant to be recognized as pointing to this event, outside the play world. While it seems probable that the insertion of the satyrs' dance in *The Winter's Tale* is a consequence of its success in *The Masque of Oberon*, this does not help us to fix the date after which the play must have been written, for the dance, with the lines leading up to it (322–39), may well have been inserted at a later date. There are, indeed, a few pointers in the text that this is, in fact, what happened (see Allardyce Nicoll's discussion in *Shakespeare Jahrbuch*, XCIV, 1958, 56–7).

336   *by th'square* precisely

340   *O, father, you'll know more of that hereafter.* Polixenes has been continuing his *sad talk* (line 308) with the old Shepherd.

342   *He's simple and tells much.* This plainly refers not to Florizel, as has been claimed, but to the old Shepherd,

whom he has been sounding on the subject of the lovers.

345   *handed* had to do with

346   *knacks* knick-knacks

349   *nothing marted* made no deal

350   *Interpretation should abuse* should misinterpret

351   *straited* at a loss

352–3   *if you make a care | Of happy holding her* if you are concerned to keep her happy

355   *looks* looks for

356–7   *which I have given already, | But not delivered.* Florizel is distinguishing between the free gift of his heart and the formal handing over of it, 'delivery' as a legal term being 'the formal transfer of a deed by the grantor'. The attempted marriage contract that follows is to be this 'delivery'.

358   *Before this ancient sir.* The dramatic irony of the scene requires, and the lines that follow make clear, that this refers to Polixenes and not, as some commentators have argued, to Camillo.

       whom, it should seem. Shakespeare frequently uses *whom* where we should use 'who'.

361   *bolted* sifted

364   *was* that was

371   *force* physical strength

374–5   *Commend them and condemn them to her service | Or to their own perdition* commend them to her service or condemn them to their own complete ruin

386   *Enough then for your wonder* (probably 'enough to amaze you even then' (when you know who I am))

387   *Contract us 'fore these witnesses.* There were two kinds of marriage contracts in Shakespeare's time: *per verba de futuro* (in which the couple engaged themselves to become husband and wife at a future date), a contract which could be dissolved for a variety of reasons; and *per verba de praesenti* (in which the couple declared that henceforth they were husband and wife), a con-

tract which constituted a legally binding marriage.
The interruption through Polixenes makes it impossible to discover which of the two it was to be, though
his reference to *nuptial* (line 392) suggests that Shakespeare thought of it as a *de praesenti* contract.

396 *altering rheums* catarrhs which affect his mind

397 *Dispute his own estate* discuss his own affairs

399 *being childish* when a child

403 *Something* somewhat
     Reason it is reasonable that

417 *affects* aims at, aspires to

420 *of force* of necessity

421 *cop'st with* have to do with

423 *fond* foolish

425 *knack* trifle, toy

428 *Far* farther (like 'near', 'far' could also be used for the
     comparative)
     Deucalion (the equivalent in Greek mythology to
     Noah)

431 *dead* deadly, mortal

432-4 *yea, him too, | That makes himself, but for our honour
       therein, | Unworthy thee.* Probably Polixenes is using
       the plural of majesty, *honour* having here the rare
       meaning of 'exalted position': 'yea, worthy of him
       too, who makes himself unworthy of thee (by the
       nature of his actions), if my exalted position were not
       involved.'

440 *him* (Polixenes)

448 *Speak ere thou die'st.* Neither Camillo nor the Shep-
     herd (lines 453-5) seems to have taken in the King's
     words of reprieve (lines 429-31).

455 *Where no priest shovels in dust.* Hanged men were
     buried under the gallows, without a funeral service.

457 *mingle faith* join in a pledge (of marriage)

462-3 *More straining on for plucking back, not following | My
       leash unwillingly.* Florizel sees himself as a hound on a
       leash, all the more eager to pursue his course for being

216

plucked back, refusing to let himself unwillingly be dragged off by his master.

468   *highness* (probably 'haughtiness' rather than the title)

470   *I think Camillo?* Perhaps Camillo is just beginning to remove his disguise and becomes therefore recognizable (the convention being that all disguise is impenetrable).

475–6   *Let Nature crush the sides o'th'earth together | And mar the seeds within!* All material substances were believed to be derived from 'seeds' (called 'germens' in *Macbeth*, IV.1.58 and *King Lear*, III.2.8). Nature would thus be destroying not only all actual but also all potential life on earth.

478   *affection.* The word had much stronger meanings in Shakespeare's time than it has now. It could signify 'sexual desire', as at I.2.138, or 'passionate love', as here.

479   *fancy* love

490   *As you've e'er been my father's honoured friend.* F reads *As you haue euer bin my Fathers honour'd friend*, which is metrically quite un-Shakespearian; later Folios omitted *honour'd*. The elisions here adopted are a less drastic attempt to restore the metre. It seems far more probable that the scribe or compositor ignored Shakespeare's elisions than that he added an adjective not found in the manuscript.

494   *Tug* contend

497   *opportune* (stressed on the second syllable)

500–   *benefit your knowledge, nor | Concern me the reporting*
501   profit you to know, nor is it for me to tell

502   *easier for* more open to

504   *irremovable* immovable. The word may here, as often with Shakespeare, be used adverbially: 'He's immovably resolved for flight.' F's comma after *irremovable* means little, since commas are found in the oddest places throughout the Folio text of the play (for instance, two lines later F prints a comma after *going*).

510–12 *Now, good Camillo, | I am so fraught with curious busi-ness that | I leave out ceremony.* Florizel is apologizing for talking apart to Perdita in Camillo's presence, a breach of courtesy which derives from Shakespeare's need to let Camillo reveal his thoughts to the audience (compare the note to line 656).

511 *curious* causing anxiety, worrying

517 *as thought on* as fully as they are borne in mind

520–22 *direction. | If . . . | . . . alteration, on. . . .* F punctuates *direction, | If . . . | . . . alteration. On. . . .* This punctuation is certainly possible, and a number of editors have adopted it. But the two conditional clauses in one sentence are awkward, and the verse as here punctuated (in accord with most editors since Pope) sounds more Shakespearian.

521 *ponderous* of great import

524 *become your highness* accord with your high station

528–9 *And, with my best endeavours in your absence, | Your discontenting father strive to qualify.* Commentators are divided on whether this means 'and where, together with my best endeavours in your absence, you may strive to appease your angry father' or 'and with my best endeavours in your absence *I shall* strive to appease your angry father'. The syntax strongly suggests that the former represents Shakespeare's meaning, and the passage has been punctuated accordingly. The implication seems to be that Florizel could make use of the power of intercession with Polixenes that Leontes can command.

529 *discontenting* vexed, angry
qualify appease

530 *bring him up to liking* get him to the point of approving

535–6 *But as th'unthought-on accident is guilty | To what we wildly do* but as the unexpected accident (the intervention by Polixenes) is responsible for what we rashly are about to do

545 *free* noble

546   *asks thee, the son, forgiveness.* A number of recent
editors have adhered to F's *asks thee there Sonne for-
giuenesse*, punctuating 'asks thee there "Son, forgiveness!"' or 'asks thee there, son, forgiveness'. This
reading seems, however, very forced and implausible.
The emendation first introduced in the third Folio,
and accepted by most editors, has therefore been
adopted.

548   *fresh* young and lovely

548-9   *o'er and o'er divides him | 'Twixt his unkindness and his
kindness* keeps on talking in turn of his (former)
wicked behaviour (towards Polixenes) and his (present)
love (for him and you)

556   *deliver* say

558   *The which shall point you forth at every sitting* which
shall indicate to you at every meeting

560   *bosom* intimate thoughts

574   *take in* conquer, subdue

575   *these seven years.* This is a proverbial expression,
signifying 'for a very long time'.

        seven (here monosyllabic)

577-8   *She is as forward of her breeding as | She is i'th'rear' our
birth* she is as much above her upbringing as she is
below me in birth. The apostrophe after *rear*, taken
over from F, indicates that a word ('of') has been
omitted.

584   *medicine.* The word could also mean 'physician' (from
French *médecin*), and this may, but need not, be its
meaning here.

586   *appear* appear as such

587   *fortunes* possessions, wealth

589   *royally appointed* equipped like royalty

590   *scene* stage performance

595   *table-book* a pocket notebook

597   *fasting* being empty

598   *a benediction* blessedness

599-600 *best in picture.* No parallel usage has been traced, pre-

sumably because it is a nonce-use, coined to suggest
punningly 'best looking' (because fattest) and hence
'best to pick'.

603   *pettitoes* pigs' trotters (but also used jestingly of human
feet)

605   *stuck in ears* went to their ears, became hearing

606   *placket*. See note on lines 242–3 of this scene.

606–7   *to geld a codpiece of a purse* to cut off a purse from the
bag-like appendage worn in the front of breeches in
Shakespeare's day

608   *my sir's* (the Clown's)

609   *nothing* nothingness

610   *festival* (adjective) brought for the feast

621   *Nothing may* nothing that may

623   *hanging* (the punishment in Shakespeare's day for any
theft over twelve pence in value)

624–5   *How now, good fellow! Why shak'st thou so? Fear not,
man: here's no harm intended to thee.* F sets this out as
verse, and is followed by many editors. But it is clearly
meant to be prose, the medium in which Camillo talks
with Autolycus throughout.

629   *discase* undress

630   *thou must think* you must realize

631–2   *Though the pennyworth on his side be the worst* though he
gets the worst of the exchange

632–3   *some boot* something into the bargain

637   *flayed* skinned (undressed)

641   *earnest* money in part payment (the *boot* of line 633).
A quibble on the *earnest* of line 638.

644   *my prophecy* (the prophecy he just made in calling her
Fortunate)

648–9   *Dismantle you, and, as you can, disliken | The truth of
your own seeming* remove your outer garment (presumably the *unusual weeds* referred to in line 1), and
make yourself as unlike your true appearance as you
can

650   *eyes over* spying eyes (compare IV.2.35)

656 *what have we twain forgot!* (a mere device to get them out of the way so that Camillo can deliver his aside; hence we must not ask what it was that they had forgot)

674–5 *with his clog at his heels* (an ungallant reference to Perdita)

675–8 *If I thought it were a piece of honesty to acquaint the King withal, I would not do't. I hold it the more knavery to conceal it; and therein am I constant to my profession.* The lines have been much emended, since, as they stand, the argument is somewhat baffling. The illogicality seems due to excessive compression, which has led to the omission of one of the links in the chain of reasoning, to the effect that, since it would be a piece of knavery towards Florizel to reveal it to the King, he may do so; but as it is even more knavish to conceal it, this is what he will do.

678 *profession* avowed practice

679 *hot* keen

683 *changeling.* See note on III.3.114–15.

687 *Go to* go on

692 *all but what she has with her.* This presumably refers to Hermione's jewel, which Perdita wore about the neck when she was found (see V.2.33), and which she has, it seems, put on for the feast.

700 *by I know not how much an ounce.* The majority of editors have adhered to F's reading *by I know how much an ounce,* claiming that this makes adequate sense if the Clown's assertion is accompanied by a knowing wink. But this explanation seems very strained, and the insertion of 'not', first made by eighteenth-century editors, fully justified.

705 *my master.* Autolycus had been in Florizel's service (see IV.3.13) and still thinks of him as his master.

709 *excrement* outgrowth (here the false beard that Autolycus wears in his pedlar's disguise)

713 *condition* nature

714 *having* property

717   *A lie : you are rough and hairy.* One of the meanings of
        plain was 'smooth'. Autolycus pretends to understand
        the word in this sense.

718–21 *it becomes none but tradesmen, and they often give us*
        soldiers the lie ; but we pay them for it with stamped coin,
        not stabbing steel ; therefore they do not give us the lie.
        Tradesmen give soldiers the lie in the sense of lying to
        them about their wares. But they are paid for it with
        good money (*stamped coin*), not with *stabbing steel* (the
        soldier's retort to being given the lie in the usual
        sense, that of being accused to his face of lying).
        Hence tradesmen do not *give* soldiers the lie, they *sell*
        it (the stress in the last sentence falls on *give*).

722–3   *Your worship had like to have given us one, if you had not*
        taken yourself with the manner. This puzzling remark
        has been variously explained. Most probably the
        Clown is saying: 'Your worship would have told *us* an
        untruth (when you claimed that tradesmen often
        accuse soldiers to their face of lying), had you not
        caught yourself in the act (and changed your state-
        ment).' 'To be taken with the manner' (or 'mainour')
        is a legal phrase, meaning 'to be caught in the act of
        doing something unlawful'.

727   *measure* stately motion

730   *insinuate.* The word seems to be here used intransi-
        tively, meaning 'make my way in a sinuous or subtle
        manner'.

        to toaze. F's *at toaze* was changed in subsequent
        Folios to *or toaze*, and this reading has been adopted
        by most later editors. A more plausible emendation is,
        however, 'to toaze', meaning 'in order to tease' (a
        metaphor from the carding of wool).

731   *cap-à-pie* from top to toe

733   *open* disclose

737   *Advocate's the court-word for a pheasant.* The Clown
        thinks that, as suitors from the country, they are ex-
        pected to bring a gift of pheasants, which is what he

takes the word *advocate* to mean. Many editors quite unjustifiably emend *pheasant* to 'present', and assume a mishearing by the Shepherd in line 739.

740-42 *How blessed are we that are not simple men! | Yet Nature might have made me as these are : | Therefore I'll not disdain.* As part of his parody of the language of the court, Autolycus falls momentarily into blank verse. Perhaps he purposely rhymes *men* with the *hen* of the preceding line, which also happens to be blank verse.

745 *His garments are rich.* Shakespeare had probably forgotten that Florizel's garments, which Autolycus has put on, are *a swain's wearing* (IV.4.9). See note on IV.4.2-3.

747-8 *fantastical* eccentric, odd

748-9 *the picking on's teeth* the fact that he picks his teeth. The use and display of toothpicks (they were even worn in the hat) were considered the mark of a fashionable gentleman in Shakespeare's day.

752-3 *this fardel and box.* The *fardel* consists of the garments worn by the infant Perdita when found; the *box* contains presumably the remainder of the gold and the scroll left with her by Antigonus (see III.3.113-18 and V.2.33-5).

756-60 *Age, thou hast lost thy labour. . . . The King is not at the palace ; he is gone aboard a new ship, to purge melancholy and air himself.* This echoes *Pandosto*: '"But", quoth Capnio, "you lose your labour in going to the palace, for the king means this day to take the air of the sea, and to go aboard of a ship that lies in the haven"' (page 215).

764 *handfast* custody, durance

768 *wit* ingenuity

769 *germane* related

773 *offer* dare, presume

779-87 *He has a son . . . blown to death.* It is usually claimed that the description of these tortures is based on Boccaccio's story of Bernabò and Zinevra (*Decameron,*

223

II.9), which Shakespeare had read for the writing of *Cymbeline*. There the villain is tied to a post in the sun, anointed with honey, and killed and devoured to the bone by flies, wasps, and gadflies. (See *Elizabethan Love Stories*, edited by T. J. B. Spencer, Penguin Books, 1968, pages 161–75.) It is possible that Shakespeare was drawing on memories of this incident, but quite as likely that what he had in mind were reports of the cruel tortures inflicted by the Spaniards upon Negroes and American Indians. 'Drake found a negro who had been sentenced to be whipped raw, set in the sun, and tortured to death by mosquitoes. An Indian was smeared with brimstone, fired, restored to health, anointed with honey, chained to a tree, "where mosquitoes flocked about him like motes in the sun and did pitifully sting him"' (*Shakespeare's England*, Oxford University Press, Vol. I, page 185).

784   *prognostication* weather forecast for the year in the almanac

786   *he* (the sun)
      flies (any winged insects)

787   *blown*. The few editors who comment on the word at all explain its meaning as 'filled with eggs' or 'befouled'. But this seems a very improbable way of killing a man. It is much more likely that its meaning is 'puffed up, swollen' (through the insects' stings). Shakespeare used the word 'blow' in the sense of 'puff up' in *Twelfth Night*, II.5.41–2 ('Look how imagination blows him') and probably also, in connexion with flies' stings, in *Antony and Cleopatra*, V.2.59–60 ('and let the water-flies | Blow me into abhorring').

790   *what you have to the King* what your business is with the King

790–91 *something gently considered* rather generously remunerated

795–6   *Close with him* accept his offer

796   *and though* even though

808–9 *though my case be a pitiful one, I hope I shall not be flayed out of it.* The Clown puns on two meanings of *case*: 'plight' and 'covering' or 'skin'.

815 *gone* lost

819–20 *look upon the hedge* relieve myself

826–7 *I am courted now with a double occasion* I am wooed (by Fortune) with a twofold opportunity (of gain)

829 *turn back* redound

831 *shore them* put them ashore

832 *concerns him nothing* is of no importance to him

I.2 *sorrow* mourning

4 *penitence.* The word's primary meaning seems here to be 'penance'.

8 *in them* (probably 'in thinking of her virtues')

19 *good now* (a phrase of entreaty frequently used by Shakespeare)

25 *You pity not the state, nor the remembrance* (a zeugma) you pity not the state, nor give thought to the remembrance

27 *fail* failure

28–9 *and devour | Incertain lookers-on* (probably 'and destroy the onlookers, who will not know what to do')

30 *is well.* The phrase is repeatedly used by Shakespeare to describe the state of the dead.

35 *Respecting* in comparison with

36 *Will* are determined to

48 *successor.* The stress falls on the first syllable.

52 *squared me to* let myself be ruled by

59 *Where we offenders move, appear soul-vexed.* F reads (*Where we Offendors now appeare*) *Soule-vext.* Of the many emendations that have been proposed the one here adopted seems the most Shakespearian and plausible (*move* in the manuscript could easily have been misread as *now*).

60 *Why to me?* why is this insult offered to me?

61   *incense* incite, stir up

66   *rift* split

67   *mine* my eyes

73   *tempt* try, put to the test

75   *Affront* confront

84   (stage direction) *Enter a Gentleman.* F's *Enter a Seruant* has been altered, as it is likely to mislead the modern reader. It is, however, not inaccurate, since a gentleman in the king's service could be so described.

88   *What with him?* what are those with him? (The question is repeated four lines later in *What train?*)

89   *Like to* in a manner appropriate to

90   *out of circumstance* without ceremony

91   *framed* designed

97   *so must thy grave* so must you, now that you are in your grave

100   *Is colder than that theme* is colder than the subject of your verses is (now that she is dead)

100– *she had not been, | Nor was not to be, equalled.* Since the
101   eighteenth century, editors have put these words in inverted commas, claiming them to be an extract from the Gentleman's verse. But the tenses prove this to be mistaken (what the Gentleman must have written is 'she has not been, nor is not to be, equalled'), and make clear that Paulina is not quoting his exact words. This edition, therefore, follows F in omitting the inverted commas.

102   *shrewdly* mightily

108   *professors* those who proclaim their adherence to a religion

109   *Not women!* Editors follow F in placing a question mark after *women*. But Paulina is exclaiming 'This surely does not apply to women!' In Elizabethan punctuation the question mark often stands for an exclamation mark.

113   *assisted with* accompanied by

135   *brave* noble

135-7   *whom, | Though bearing misery, I desire my life | Once more to look on him* to look on whom once more I desire to go on living, though my life is one of misery (*him* is redundant)

139   *at friend* in the way of friendship

140-42   *and but infirmity, | Which waits upon worn times, hath something seized | His wished ability* and were it not that infirmity, which attends old age, has to some extent taken prisoner the ability he desires to have

148   *offices* kindnesses

149   *rarely* exceptionally

149-50   *are as interpreters | Of my behindhand slackness* make manifest how slack I have been (in my *offices* towards him)

155   *adventure* hazard

156   *Smalus.* Shakespeare seems to have derived this name, like several others in the play, from Plutarch, who, in the Life of Dion, speaks of a voyage from Libya to a village in Sicily which is governed by a Carthaginian captain called Synalus. *Smalus* may be the scribe's or compositor's misreading of that name.

158-9   *whose daughter | His tears proclaimed his, parting with her* whose tears, when he was parting with her, proclaimed her to be his daughter

160   *friendly* being favourable

164   *Who for Bohemia bend* and they are now making for Bohemia

169   *climate here* dwell in this country

170   *graceful* full of divine grace

175-7   *What might I have been, | Might I a son and daughter now have looked on, | Such goodly things as you!* We have here one of the many touches of dramatic irony in this scene, an irony which is heightened through the Elizabethan usage of 'son' and 'daughter' for 'son-in-law' and 'daughter-in-law' (a usage which forms the basis of Florizel's reply in lines 207-8).

181   *attach* seize, arrest

182   *His dignity and duty both cast off* having thrown off his dignity as a prince and his duty as a son

186-7   *it becomes | My marvel* it befits my astonishment

197   *Has ... in question* is interrogating

206   *The odds for high and low's alike.* Many different explanations of this line have been given. The most probable meaning is: 'The odds on high and low being united in marriage are similar to those on the stars kissing the valleys'. Less plausible, because much less closely related to the thought of the immediately preceding lines, are the meanings 'The odds (for a happy issue) are the same for high-born and low-born' (in other words, 'My being a king's son does not make Fortune favour me'), and 'The odds for high and low numbers coming up in the game of dice (which life is) are the same' (in other words, 'We are entirely in the hands of Fortune').

213   *worth* rank

215-16   *Though Fortune, visible an enemy, | Should chase us, with my father* (probably 'though Fortune were actually to be seen as an enemy pursuing us, together with my father')

218-19   *Remember since you owed no more to Time | Than I do now* remember the days when you were no older than I am now

222-3   *Would he do so, I'd beg your precious mistress, | Which he counts but a trifle.* What in *Pandosto* is a violent and protracted passion (see Introduction, page 11) has been reduced by Shakespeare to a moment of amiable banter.

V.2.9   *broken delivery* disjointed account

11   *notes of admiration* marks of wonder (as *notes of admiration* could also mean 'exclamation marks', a quibble may be intended)

17   *seeing* what he saw

18   *importance* import, meaning

18–19   *the extremity of the one* the utmost degree of one or the other

24–5   *that ballad-makers cannot be able to express it.* See note to IV.4.260–79.

30–31   *pregnant by circumstance* clear through circumstantial evidence

33–4   *the letters of Antigonus* what has been written by Antigonus

35   *character* handwriting

36   *affection of* bent towards

46   *countenance* bearing, demeanour

48   *favour* look, appearance

52   *clipping* embracing

54   *like a weather-bitten conduit of many kings' reigns* like a weather-worn water-spout which has seen the reigns of many kings (the tears flowing down the old Shepherd's face prompt the image of the water-spout, which, on large medieval buildings, was often in the form of an old man's head; there may also be a pun on *reigns*)

56   *undoes description to do it* beggars description to paint it

60   *rehearse* relate, narrate

62–3   *innocence* guilelessness

72–3   *She had one eye declined for the loss of her husband, another elevated that the oracle was fulfilled.* The expression 'to cry (or look down) with one eye and laugh (or look up) with the other', meaning 'to experience a mixture of grief and joy', was proverbial. A version of it is found in Claudius's 'With an auspicious and a dropping eye' (*Hamlet*, I.2.11). It seems most unlikely that Shakespeare meant this description of Paulina to have a comic effect, as has been claimed.

76   *losing* being lost

77   *act.* The primary meaning is evidently 'that which took place' (referring not merely to Paulina's actions but to everything that has been described). But the further, obsolete, meaning of 'performance of part of a

play' is also present, and is responsible for the play-house-metaphors in the rest of the sentence.

86   *dolour* grief

88   *Who was most marble* even the most hard-hearted

93–5   *a piece many years in doing and now newly performed by that rare Italian master, Julio Romano.* This is Shakespeare's most celebrated anachronism, in a play which is full of similar, if less glaring, anachronisms. The fact that Shakespeare turned Giulio Romano (died 1546) into a sculptor, when he was widely known only as a painter, may be due either to ignorance (Shakespeare, having heard of him as a famous painter, just assuming that he was also a sculptor) or to learning. For in Vasari's *Lives of . . . Painters* he would have found the following Latin epitaph for Giulio: 'Jupiter saw sculptured and painted statues breathe and earthly buildings made equal to those in heaven by the skill of Giulio Romano'. If Shakespeare had read these lines they may, in fact, have determined his choice of Giulio as the sculptor who so perfectly is Nature's ape. Yet there is the alternative possibility that Shakespeare thought of Giulio as merely having painted the statue, which had been carved by someone else. In that case *performed* may have not just the meaning of 'carried through to completion' but the more specific one (already, it seems, obsolete by 1611) of 'completed by adding what is wanting'. However, the praise of Giulio as Nature's ape seems far more appropriate if he is thought of as not only the statue's painter but also its sculptor.

97   *beguile Nature of her custom* rob Nature of her trade

100   *greediness of affection* eager desire

106   *piece* augment, add to

109–10 *unthrifty to our knowledge* wasting the opportunity to increase our knowledge

120   *relished* found acceptance

125   *gentlemen born.* To be officially accepted as a 'gentle-

man born' in Shakespeare's day, one had to be descended from three degrees of gentry on both sides.

130 *Give me the lie.* When accused to his face of lying, a gentleman's honour required him to fight (see *As You Like It*, V.4.44 ff.).

143–4 *preposterous* (a malapropism for 'prosperous')

148 *gentle* kind, generous (a characteristic contrast between father and son: where for the Clown the chief marks of the gentleman are his fine clothes and his readiness to fight and swear, for the old Shepherd they are generosity and courtesy)

151 *an it like* if it please

155 *Not swear it, now I am a gentleman?* Swearing, like duelling, was held to be the prerogative of gentlemen.

155–6 *boors and franklins* peasants and yeomen

160 *a tall fellow of thy hands* a valiant fellow in a fight

164 *I will prove so, sir, to my power.* No doubt Autolycus is secretly making his promise refer to his valiant use of his hands as a cut-purse and pick-pocket. We are clearly not meant to think of him as in any way reformed at the end of the play.

169 *picture* sculptured figure, effigy

.3.1 *grave* (probably here 'having weight and importance', rather than 'of a dignified and serious demeanour')

4 *paid home* amply repaid

9 *We honour you with trouble* (probably 'Our visit, which you call an honour, is really a trouble')

12 *singularities* rarities, curiosities

18 *Lonely* isolated. F's *Louely* has found its defenders, but most editors since the eighteenth century have rightly chosen to emend.

19 *as lively mocked* as closely counterfeited

25 *Hermione.* The name, which normally in the play has four syllables, is here and in line 28 reduced to three, the 'o' being scarcely sounded.

38   *piece* work of art

41   *admiring* filled with wonder

47   *The statue is but newly fixed* the colours of the statue
      have only just been made fast

49   *sore* heavily, thickly (the metaphor here and in the next
      two lines comes from painting, inspired, no doubt, by
      the immediately preceding lines)

56   *piece up* add to (his own store of grief)

57   *image* statue

58   *wrought* moved, affected

62   *Would I were dead but that methinks already* may I die
      if it does not seem to me already (that it moves)

67   *fixure* (an earlier form of 'fixture')

68   *As* so that

72   *No settled senses of the world* no calm mind in the world

83   *painting* paint

85   *forbear* withdraw

86   *presently* immediately

96   *Or those.* F's *On: those* has been retained and defended
      by some editors; but the emendation to *Or those*,
      generally adopted since the eighteenth century, is
      almost certainly correct.

100   *look upon* look on

105–7 *Do not shun her | Until you see her die again, for then |
      You kill her double.* This is oddly phrased, but must
      mean 'If you shun her now, you will kill her a second
      time'.

107   *double* a second time

125–8 *For thou shalt hear that I, | Knowing by Paulina that the
      oracle | Gave hope thou wast in being, have preserved |
      Myself to see the issue.* This is the only explanation of
      Hermione's sixteen-year-long sequestration that
      Shakespeare provides, and not a few readers have felt
      that he ought to have thought up a better one. Cole-
      ridge declared that 'it seems a mere indolence of the
      great bard not to have provided in the oracular re-
      sponse ... some ground for Hermione's seeming

death and fifteen years voluntary concealment. This
might have been easily effected by some obscure sentence of the oracle, as for example: "Nor shall he ever
recover an heir, if he have a wife before that recovery."' In fact, Shakespeare needed only to change
one word in the oracle, making its last sentence read,
'and the King shall live without a *wife*, if that which is
lost be not found'.

126   *Knowing by Paulina.* Shakespeare appears to have forgotten that Hermione was present when the oracle was
read.

129   *upon this push* (probably 'at this moment of stress')

130   *with like relation.* The meaning seems to be not, as
most commentators claim, 'by telling their stories too',
but rather 'by asking you similarly to tell your story'.

132   *Partake* impart, make known
turtle. See note on IV.4.154–5.

135   *till I am lost* till I perish

142   *For* as for

144   *whose worth and honesty.* This undoubtedly refers not
to Paulina, as has been claimed, but to Camillo.

145   *richly noted* abundantly well known
justified affirmed

149   *This' your son-in-law.* The apostrophe, absent in F, has
been inserted to mark the omission of 'is', a contrac-
tion frequently used by Shakespeare and his contemporaries.

151   *troth-plight* betrothed

AN ACCOUNT OF THE TEXT

The Winter's Tale was published for the first time in 1623, in
the collected edition of Shakespeare's plays known as the first
Folio. All subsequent editions of it derive from this text, which
is therefore our only authority for what Shakespeare wrote.
Fortunately it is an exceptionally good text, with very few signs
of corruption. The copy used by the printer seems to have been
a transcript made by Ralph Crane, a professional scribe, who
was sometimes employed as copyist by the King's Men,
Shakespeare's company. The Folio text of *The Winter's Tale*
has all the marks of Crane's transcripts:

1. The lavish use of brackets, apostrophes, and hyphens.

2. The full division of the play into Acts and scenes. This
division has been adopted by most subsequent editors, though
some, chiefly in the eighteenth century, have departed from it
by leaving F's IV.1 (the chorus-speech of Time) unnumbered,
so that their IV.1, IV.2, and IV.3 are F's (and our) IV.2, IV.3,
and IV.4.

3. The use of so-called 'massed entries', that is a listing in the
scene heading of all the characters appearing in the course of
that scene, whether they are present from the beginning or not.
For instance, F's scene heading for II.1 reads *Enter Hermione,
Mamillius, Ladies: Leontes, Antigonus, Lords.*, though Leontes,
Antigonus, and Lords do not enter until line 32. But the use of
massed entries is not consistent: they are not found in two
scenes, IV.3 and V.2, where the entries are given in the normal
manner; and sometimes the entrance of characters listed in the
massed entry is also marked at its proper place within the scene,
though more often it is not.

4. The paucity of stage directions. The few directions which
are to be found consist of a bare listing of exits and entrances

(with the exceptions listed on pages 238–9). Most of the stage directions in our text are therefore editorial additions.

Whether Crane's transcript was made from Shakespeare's own manuscript ('foul papers') is uncertain. Whatever its derivation, it must have been a legible and clean text, which set the copyist few problems. We know, however, for certain that the company's prompt-book of *The Winter's Tale* had got lost by the summer of 1623, and that there was some delay in printing the play at the end of the Comedy section of the Folio. The most cogent and economical hypothesis seems, therefore, that when it was the turn of *The Winter's Tale* to be printed, in the autumn of 1621, the loss of the prompt-book was discovered and that Ralph Crane was commissioned to make a transcript, from Shakespeare's own manuscript or a clean copy of it.

The Winter's Tale is one of seven plays in the first Folio which provide a list of the characters in the play. It is printed at the end of the text and reads as follows:

The Names of the Actors.

Leontes, King of Sicillia.
Mamillus, yong Prince of Sicillia.
Camillo.
Antigonus.   *Foure*
Cleomines.   *Lords of Sicillia.*
Dion.
Hermione, Queene to Leontes.
Perdita, Daughter to Leontes and Hermione.
Paulina, wife to Antigonus.
Emilia, a Lady.
Polixenes, King of Bohemia.
Florizell, Prince of Bohemia.
Old Shepheard, reputed Father of Perdita.
Clowne, his Sonne.
Autolicus, a Rogue.
Archidamus, a Lord of Bohemia.
Other Lords, and Gentlemen, and Seruants.
Shepheards, and Shephearddesses.

COLLATIONS

I

The following is a list of readings in the present text of *The Winter's Tale* which differ significantly from those found in F (F's reading is printed on the right of the square brackets, in the original spelling, except that the 'long s' [ʃ] has been replaced by 's'). Most of these emendations were introduced by eighteenth-century editors. Those marked with an asterisk are discussed in the Commentary. Purely typographical errors in F have not been listed.

I.2.	104	And] A
	*148	What] *Leo.* What
	*208	you, they say] you say
	276	hobby-horse] Holy-Horse
	*337	forsealing] for sealing
	377–8	and dare not | Be intelligent to me?] and dare not? | Be intelligent to me,
II.1.	*90	fedary] Federarie
	*143	lam-damn] Land-damne
2.	53	let't] le't
3.	39	What] Who
	*177	its] it
III.2.	*10	Silence!] *Silence.*
	32	Who] Whom
	99	its] it
3.	28	thrower-out] Thower-out
	*116	made] mad
IV.3.	*10	With heigh, with heigh,] *With heigh,*
4.	*12	Digest it with accustom] Digest with a Custome
	*13	swoon] sworne
	160	out] on't
	245	kiln-hole] kill-hole
	308	gentlemen] Gent.
	416	acknowledged] acknowledge

IV .4.   420 who] whom
          425 shalt sce] shalt neuer see
          436 hoop] hope
          464 your] my
        *490 As you've e'cr] As you haue euer
          497 our] her
        *546 thee, the son,] thee there Sonne
          577 She is as] She's as
          607 filed keys off] fill'd Keyes of
          637 flayed] fled
        *700 know not] know
        *730 to toazc] at toaze
          739 pheasant, cock nor hen] Pheazant Cock, nor Hen
          742 I'll] I will

V.1.   12 of. PAULINA True, too true,] of, true. *Paul.* Too
               true
        *59 Where we offenders move, appear soul-vexed,]
               (Where we Offendors now appeare) Soule-vext,
          61 just cause] iust such cause
          75 CLEOMENES Good madam – PAULINA I have
               done] *Cleo.* Good Madame, I haue done

V.3.   *18 Lonely] Louely
          *96 Or those] On: those

2

The following is a list of the only stage directions (other than
simple exits and entrances) that appear in F. Other stage
directions in this edition are editorial additions.

III.2.   o Enter Leontes, Lords, Officers: Hermione (as to
               her Triall) Ladies: Cleomines, Dion.
III.3.   57 Exit pursued by a Beare.
IV.1.   o Enter Time, the Chorus.
IV.3.   o Enter Autolicus singing.
IV.4.   167 Heere a Daunce of Shepheards and Shep-
               hearddesses.

219 Enter Autolicus singing.

339 Heere a Dance of twelue Satyres.

V.3. 0 Enter Leontes, Polixenes, Florizell, Perdita, Camillo, Paulina: Hermione (like a Statue:) Lords, &c.

THE SONGS

THERE are six songs in *The Winter's Tale*, all of them sung by Autolycus (one as a three-part song with Dorcas and Mopsa). For three of these the earliest settings that have been preserved belong to the mid eighteenth century: those for 'When daffodils begin to peer' (IV.3.1) and 'Will you buy any tape' (IV.4.313) are by William Boyce (about 1759 and 1769); that for 'But shall I go mourn for that, my dear?' (IV.3.15) is by J. F. Lampe (about 1745). For the other three songs earlier settings have come down to us. They are printed below, in transcriptions made for this edition by Dr F. W. Sternfeld. The tune of 'Jog on, jog on, the footpath way' (IV.3.121) is found first in the second decade of the seventeenth century, arranged in a set of variations by Richard Farnaby, in the Fitzwilliam Virginal Book. The version here given follows the text in Playford's *Musical Companion* (1667), except for two small variants, which have been taken from the Fitzwilliam Virginal Book. The tune of 'Lawn as white as driven snow' (IV.4.220) was printed for the first time in John Wilson's *Cheerful Airs or Ballads* (1659). It is possible that this setting is Wilson's arrangement of the original tune. For 'Get you hence, for I must go' (IV.4.295) two early settings are extant. The first, which is here transcribed, is found in a manuscript (New York Public Library, Drexel 4175) of the first half of the seventeenth century, and has an accompaniment in lyra-viol tablature. The second, found in a manuscript of about 1640, consists of the same melody transposed to another key. Instead of the lyra-viol tablature it has a thoroughbass accompaniment. This setting is incomplete, ending after 'if to either thou dost ill'.

1. 'Jog on, jog on, the footpath way' (IV.3.121).

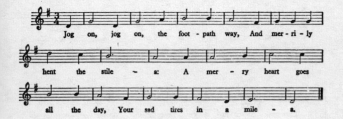

Jog on, jog on, the foot - path way, And mer - ri - ly hent the stile - a: A mer - ry heart goes all the day, Your sad tires in a mile - a.

2. 'Lawn as white as driven snow' (IV.4.220).

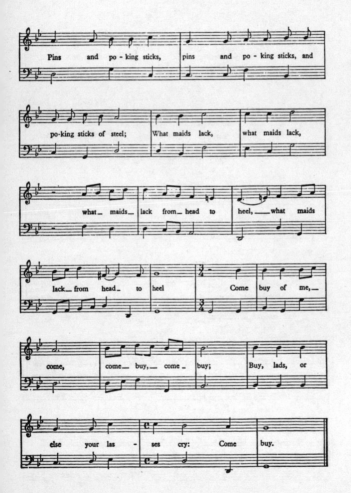

3. 'Get you hence, for I must go' (IV.4.295).

READ MORE IN PENGUIN

**ROYAL
SHAKESPEARE
COMPANY**

The Royal Shakespeare Company today is probably one of the best-known theatre companies in the world, playing regularly to audiences of more than a million people a year. The RSC has three theatres in Stratford-upon-Avon, the Royal Shakespeare Theatre, the Swan Theatre and The Other Place, and two theatres in London's Barbican Centre, the Barbican Theatre and The Pit. The Company also has an annual season in Newcastle-upon-Tyne and regularly undertakes tours throughout the UK and overseas.

Find out more about the RSC and its current repertoire by joining the Company's mailing list. Not only will you receive advance information of all the Company's activities, but also priority booking, special ticket offers, copies of the RSC Magazine and special offers on RSC publications and merchandise.

If you would like to receive details of the Company's work and an application form for the mailing list please write to:

RSC Membership Office
Royal Shakespeare Theatre
FREEPOST
Stratford-upon-Avon
CV37 6BR

or telephone: 01789 205301

READ MORE IN PENGUIN

LITERARY CRITICISM

The Penguin History of Literature

Published in ten volumes, *The Penguin History of Literature* is a superb critical survey of the English and American literature covering fourteen centuries, from the Anglo-Saxons to the present, and written by some of the most distinguished academics in their fields.

New Bearings in English Poetry F. R. Leavis

'*New Bearings in English Poetry* was the first intelligent account of the work of Eliot, Pound and Gerard Manley Hopkins to appear in English and it significantly altered critical awareness . . . Leavis gave to literary criticism a thoroughness and respectability that has never since been equalled' Peter Ackroyd, *Spectator*. 'The most influential literary critic of modern times' *Financial Times*

The Uses of Literacy Richard Hoggart

Mass literacy has opened new worlds to new readers. How far has it also been exploited to debase standards and behaviour? 'A vivid inside view of working-class culture and one of the most influential books of the post-war era' *Observer*

Epistemology of the Closet Eve Kosofsky Sedgwick

Through her brilliant interpretation of the readings of Henry James, Melville, Nietzsche, Proust and Oscar Wilde, Eve Kosofsky Sedgwick shows how questions of sexual definition are at the heart of every form of representation in this century. 'A signal event in the history of late-twentieth-century gay studies' Wayne Koestenbaum

Dangerous Pilgrimages Malcolm Bradbury

'This capacious book tracks Henry James from New England to Rye; Evelyn Waugh to a Hollywood as grotesque as he expected; Gertrude Stein to Spain to be mistaken for a bishop; Oscar Wilde to a rickety stage in Leadsville, Colorado . . . The textbook on the the transatlantic theme' *Guardian*

READ MORE IN PENGUIN

LITERARY CRITICISM

The Practice of Writing   David Lodge

This lively collection examines the work of authors ranging from the two Amises to Nabokov and Pinter; the links between private lives and published works; and the different techniques required in novels, stage plays and screenplays. 'These essays, so easy in manner, so well-built and informative, offer a fine blend of creative writing and criticism' *Sunday Times*

A Lover's Discourse   Roland Barthes

'May be the most detailed, painstaking anatomy of desire we are ever likely to see or need again ... The book is an ecstatic celebration of love and language ... readers interested in either or both ... will enjoy savouring its rich and dark delights' *Washington Post*

The New Pelican Guide to English Literature   Edited by Boris Ford

The indispensable critical guide to English and American literature in nine volumes, erudite yet accessible. From the ages of Chaucer and Shakespeare, via Georgian satirists and Victorian social critics, to the leading writers of the twentieth century, all literary life is here.

The Structure of Complex Words   William Empson

'Twentieth-century England's greatest critic after T. S. Eliot, but whereas Eliot was the high priest, Empson was the *enfant terrible* ... *The Structure of Complex Words* is one of the linguistic masterpieces of the epoch, finding in the feel and tone of our speech whole sedimented social histories' *Guardian*

Vamps and Tramps   Camille Paglia

'Paglia is a genuinely unconventional thinker ... Taken as a whole, the book gives an exceptionally interesting perspective on the last thirty years of intellectual life in America, and is, in its wacky way, a celebration of passion and the pursuit of truth' *Sunday Telegraph*

READ MORE IN PENGUIN

CRITICAL STUDIES

Described by *The Times Educational Supplement* as 'admirable' and 'superb', Penguin Critical Studies is a specially developed series of critical essays on the major works of literature for use by students in universities, colleges and schools.

Titles published or in preparation include:

SHAKESPEARE

As You Like It
Hamlet
King Lear
Macbeth
The Merchant of Venice
A Midsummer Night's Dream
Much Ado about Nothing
Othello
Shakespeare's History Plays
The Taming of the Shrew
The Tempest
Twelfth Night
The Winter's Tale

CHAUCER

Chaucer
The Prologue to
    The Canterbury Tales

SELECTION OF PLAYS

Edward Albee	**Who's Afraid of Virginia Woolf?**
Alan Ayckbourn	**Joking Apart and Other Plays**
James Baldwin	**The Amen Corner**
Bertolt Brecht	**Parables for the Theatre**
Albert Camus	**Caligula and Other Plays**
Anton Chekhov	**Plays (The Cherry Orchard/Three Sisters/ Ivanov/The Seagull/Uncle Vanya)**
Euripides	**Andromache/Electra/Hecabe/Suppliant Women/Trojan Women**
Henrik Ibsen	**A Doll's House/League of Youth/Lady from the Sea**
	Brand
Ben Jonson	**Every Man in his Humour/Sejanus, His Fall/ Volpone/Epicoene**
Thomas Kyd	**The Spanish Tragedie**
Mike Leigh	**Abigail's Party/Goose-Pimples**
Arthur Miller	**The Crucible**
	Death of a Salesman
Jean-Paul Sartre	**In Camera/The Respectable Prostitute/ Lucifer and the Lord**
Peter Shaffer	**Lettice and Lovage/Yonadab**
	The Royal Hunt of the Sun
	Equus
Bernard Shaw	**Plays Pleasant**
	Pygmalion
	John Bull's Other Island
Arnold Wesker	**Plays, Volumes 1-7**
Oscar Wilde	**The Importance of Being Earnest and Other Plays**
Thornton Wilder	**Our Town/The Skin of Our Teeth/The Matchmaker**
Tennessee Williams	**Cat on a Hot Tin Roof/The Milk Train Doesn't Stop Here Anymore/The Night of the Iguana**
August Wilson	**The Piano Lesson/Joe Turner's Come and Gone**

READ MORE IN PENGUIN

THE NEW PENGUIN SHAKESPEARE

All's Well That Ends Well	Barbara Everett
Antony and Cleopatra	Emrys Jones
As You Like It	H. J. Oliver
The Comedy of Errors	Stanley Wells
Coriolanus	G. R. Hibbard
Hamlet	T. J. B. Spencer
Henry IV, Part 1	P. H. Davison
Henry IV, Part 2	P. H. Davison
Henry V	A. R. Humphreys
Henry VI, Parts 1–3	Norman Sanders
(three volumes)	
Henry VIII	A. R. Humphreys
Julius Caesar	Norman Sanders
King John	R. L. Smallwood
King Lear	G. K. Hunter
Love's Labour's Lost	John Kerrigan
Macbeth	G. K. Hunter
Measure for Measure	J. M. Nosworthy
The Merchant of Venice	W. Moelwyn Merchant
The Merry Wives of Windsor	G. R. Hibbard
A Midsummer Night's Dream	Stanley Wells
Much Ado About Nothing	R. A. Foakes
The Narrative Poems	Maurice Evans
Othello	Kenneth Muir
Pericles	Philip Edwards
Richard II	Stanley Wells
Richard III	E. A. J. Honigmann
Romeo and Juliet	T. J. B. Spencer
The Sonnets *and* A Lover's Complaint	John Kerrigan
The Taming of the Shrew	G. R. Hibbard
The Tempest	Anne Barton
Timon of Athens	G. R. Hibbard
Troilus and Cressida	R. A. Foakes
Twelfth Night	M. M. Mahood
The Two Gentlemen of Verona	Norman Sanders
The Two Noble Kinsmen	N. W. Bawcutt
The Winter's Tale	Ernest Schanzer